THE
LIGHT
OF
ANCIENT ROMAN
CIVILIZATION

古罗马
文明之光

意大利那不勒斯国家考古博物馆珍藏

中华世纪坛艺术馆
北京坤远文博展览有限公司
编

上海书画出版社

目 录

2

CONTENTS

罗马—中国古代文明大事记

老子
公元前 6 世纪—前 5 世纪

孔子
公元前 551 年—前 479 年

墨子
公元前 468 年—前 376 年

周平王东迁洛邑
公元前 770 年

春秋战国（公元前 770 年—前 221 年）

罗马王政时期（公元前 753 年—公元前 509 年）

公元前 **700**	公元前 **600**	公元前 **500**

罗马建城
公元前 753 年

《十二铜表法》
公元前 450 年

古希腊哲学家苏格拉底
约公元前 470 年—公元前 399 年

致　辞

　　"古罗马文明之光：意大利那不勒斯国家考古博物馆珍藏展"是中华世纪坛艺术馆和意大利驻华大使馆及意大利驻华使馆文化处合作举办的重要展览。为此，我要对中华世纪坛艺术馆深表感谢。该展览将为中国观众开辟一扇充分认识为意大利和西方世界文化遗产奠定基础的美学和哲学的重要窗口。

　　那不勒斯国家考古博物馆以其杰出的考古收藏而闻名，是世界上最古老、最重要的考古机构之一。它的历史可以追溯到 18 世纪，最初是为了展示法尔内塞家族收藏以及从维苏威古镇出土的文物，其中法尔内塞家族藏品可能是最具标志性的古罗马时期文物收藏，也被认为是意大利文艺复兴时期文化和美学的主要灵感来源。直至今日，这些藏品仍然是博物馆的核心亮点。

　　此次在中华世纪坛艺术馆展出的艺术品拥有非凡的文化价值，不仅在于其作为文化遗产的内在传承意义，更在于其体现出的独特叙事。正如小普林尼所描述的那样，公元 79 年的维苏威火山的爆发将包括庞贝、赫库兰尼姆和斯塔比亚在内的罗马城市群淹没在火山灰层之下。得益于从18世纪开始的考古发掘工作，这些精美的工艺品能够完好无损地保存至今。在令人着迷的视觉魅力之外，这些艺术作品还让您得以一窥古罗马世界，这个在两千年前蓬勃发展的文明的文化、美学原则和信仰。本次展览通过对古罗马时代的视觉叙事，有效地强调了这一历史时期作为西方文化价值观和美感的重要参考点，以及作为我们现在所定义的古典时代的基本组成部分的重要性。

　　在这方面，展览还提供了对古罗马时代社会和文化背景的洞察，这些背景与对"美"的追求错综复杂地交织在一起。美的概念通过精心挑选的物品和艺术品得以体现，代表着古罗马生活最多样化的方面，从军事传统到烹饪实践，涵盖政治、戏剧和宗教，强调了古罗马文明的多面性。展品生动地展示了古典价值的起源，这一价值随后被意大利文艺复兴时期的大师们所接受和发展。展览中的标志性杰作，如《维纳斯的背影》和《阿斯克勒庇俄斯》，极为罕见的彩绘壁画，甚至是与日常生活相关的简单物品，都将通过文化遗产这一通用语言呈现在中国观众面前。

　　本次展览再次重申了意大利和中国这两大影响人类历史进程的重要文明之间在文化交流领域的悠久传统。

安博思

意大利驻中华人民共和国大使

秦商鞅变法
公元前 356 年

韩非子
公元前 280 年—前 233 年

董仲舒罢黜百家，独尊儒术
公元前 140 年

屈原
公元前 339 年—前 278 年

张骞出使西域
公元前 138 年

张骞（二次）使匈奴还，西域始通于汉
公元前 115 年

筑秦长城
公元前 214 年

齐设"稷下学宫"
公元前 374 年

司马迁撰写《史记》
公元前 104 年—前 91 年

秦朝（公元前 221 年—前 207 年） | 汉朝（公元前 206 年—公元 220 年）

马共和国时期（公元前 509 年—公元前 27 年）

| 元前 | 公元前 | 公元前 | 公元 |
| **00** | **300** | **200** | **10** |

希腊雕塑家普拉克西特列斯，创作古希腊最早的全裸女性人雕塑《尼多斯的阿佛洛狄忒》
元前 4 世纪

罗马共和国统一意大利
公元前 3 世纪

三次布匿战争
公元前 264 年—公元前 146 年

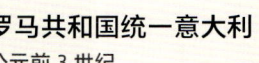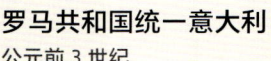

希腊哲学家柏拉图
元前 427 年—公元前 347 年

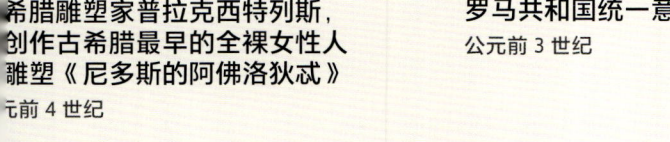

古希腊哲学家伊壁鸠鲁
公元前 341 年—公元前 270 年

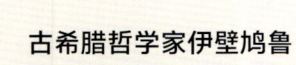

古
卢
约

古
撰

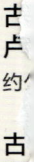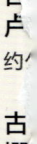

设西域都护府

公元前 60 年

东汉史学家班固，
编撰有《汉书》

公元 32 年—92 年

班超出使西域

公元 73 年

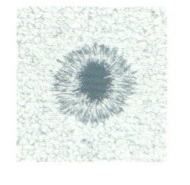

蔡伦改进造纸术

公元 105 年

《汉书》对前28年太
阳黑子的记录成为
世界上第一次对太
阳黑子的记录

公元前 28 年

甘英出使大秦——
"抵条支而历安息，
临西海以望大秦"

公元 97 年

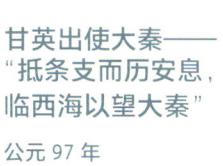

张衡造候风地动仪

公元 132 年

《九章算术》

公元 100 年左右

罗马帝国（公元前 27 年—公元 395 年）

公元 1	公元 100	公元 200

马诗人、哲学家
莱修，撰有《物性论》

元前 99 年—约公元前 55 年

马诗人维吉尔，
《埃涅阿斯记》

70 年—公元前 19 年

后三头同盟

公元前 43 年

凯撒遇刺

公元前 44 年

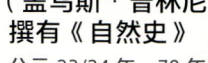

古罗马作家老普林尼
（盖乌斯·普林尼·塞孔都斯）
撰有《自然史》

公元 23/24 年—79 年

哈德良长城修建

公元 122 年

罗马皇帝路奇乌斯·维鲁斯

公元 161 年—公元 169 年在位

古罗马诗人贺拉斯，
撰有《诗艺》

元前 65 年—公元前 8 年

提图斯·李维
撰写《建城以来史》

公元前 27 年—公元 17 年

维苏威火山爆发，
庞贝与赫库兰尼
姆被火山灰掩埋

公元 79 年

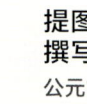

罗马皇帝马可·奥勒留

公元 161 年—公元 180 年在位

前三头同盟

元前 60 年

古罗马政治家、斯多葛学
派哲学家塞内卡，撰有
《论幸福》《论闲暇》等

公元前 4 年—公元 65 年

一队持有象牙、玳瑁的西方商人自称
受罗马皇帝马可·奥勒留派遣而来

公元 166 年

Speech

"The Light of Ancient Roman Civilization: masterpieces from the National Archaeological Museum of Naples" is an important exhibition made possible by the cooperation between the World Art Museum – to which we extend our profound gratitude – the Embassy of Italy to the People's Republic of China and the Italian Cultural Institute in Beijing. The exhibition – which has already enjoyed great success at the Museum of Art Pudong in Shanghai – is an important window into the aesthetics and philosophy, which define the cultural heritage of Italy and the Western world.

The National Archaeological Museum of Naples, renowned for its outstanding archaeological collections, stands out as one of the oldest and most significant archaeological institutions worldwide. Dating back to the 18th century, it was originally built to display the Farnese collection – probably one of the most iconic collections of Roman antiquities and a primary source of inspiration for Italian Renaissance culture and aesthetics – and the relics excavated from the ancient Vesuvian towns. To this day, these are still the Museum's core highlights.

The remarkable cultural value of the works of art now displayed at the World Art Museum resides not only in their inherent significance in terms of heritage but also in the unique narrative they embody. As described by Pliny the Younger, in 79 A.D. the eruption of Mount Vesuvius submerged a cluster of Roman cities – including Pompeii, Herculaneum, and Stabiae – beneath layers of volcanic ash. These splendid artifacts – unearthed by experts thanks to an archeological effort, which started in the 18th century – have been impeccably preserved ever since. Beyond their fascinating visual allure, these works of art offer a glimpse into the ancient Roman world, unveiling the culture, aesthetical principles, and beliefs of a civilization that thrived over two millennia ago. The exhibits encapsulate a visual narrative of the Roman era, effectively underscoring the significance of this historical period as an essential point of reference for Western cultural values and sense of beauty, and a fundamental part of what we now refer to as the classical era.

In this regard, the exhibition provides also insights into the social and cultural context of ancient Roman times, intricately intertwined and nurtured by the pursuit of "Beauty". The concept of beauty is exemplified through a refined selection of objects and artworks, all belonging to the most diverse aspects of Roman life. Ranging from military tradition to culinary practices, encompassing politics, theater and religion, the exhibition underscores the multifaceted dimensions of Roman civilization. All the items and artworks vividly showcase the origins of the classical values, later on embraced and developed by Italian Renaissance masters. Iconic masterpieces such as the Statue of Venus Callipige or the Farnese Asclepius, exceptionally rare painted frescoes, and even simple objects associated with daily life will engage the Chinese visitors through the universal language of cultural heritage.

This exhibition is an auspicious occasion to reaffirm the enduring tradition of cultural exchanges between Italy and China, two prominent civilizations that have significantly shaped the course of human history.

Massimo Ambrosetti
Ambassador of Italy to the People's Republic of China

致　辞

　　中国和意大利分处古丝绸之路两端，有着两千多年交往的历史。新时期，中意两国互为重要战略伙伴。中华世纪坛艺术馆自2001年建馆以来，与意大利文博和艺术界有着长期良好的合作，先后举办过数十场源自意大利的文化艺术展览和活动，如"罗马的曙光——意大利伊特鲁里亚文化展"，作为2006意大利文化年开篇之作的"意大利文艺复兴艺术展""伟大的世界文明"基本陈列展、"庞贝末日——源自火山喷发的故事""秦汉—罗马文明展""重返巴洛克——那不勒斯的黄金时代绘画展""回望美好时代——意大利19世纪末—20世纪初绘画精品展"等精彩项目。

　　2017年初，我馆作为首批中意两国政府确立的"中意文化合作机制"成员单位，更是开启了中意文化交流的新篇章。先后举办了"意大利文化月""彩绘地中海：一座古城的文明与幻想""拉斐尔的艺术：不可能的相遇""百年无极——西方现当代艺术大师作品展"等精彩项目。

　　作为全球最重要的考古博物馆之一，意大利那不勒斯国家考古博物馆拥有全世界范围内最完整的古罗马雕塑与庞贝古城壁画收藏。中华世纪坛艺术馆即将举办的"古罗马文明之光：意大利那不勒斯国家考古博物馆珍藏展"是这一世界顶级博物馆的代表性馆藏主题展，展览通过艺术看文明，追溯人类文明的智慧之光，精神之源。

　　走向世界，需要了解世界；走向未来，需要了解昨天。展览聚焦中西方文明交流互鉴，以"什么是美"为出发点，荟萃古罗马时期的遗珍，含雕塑、青铜器、壁画、玻璃器、马赛克等多种艺术形式，从不同方面展现古典之美，再现璀璨的古罗马文明。展览将带领中国观众回望古罗马与秦汉所处时代，了解和感知古罗马文明的艺术成就。

　　中意两国都是具有悠久历史的文明古国，各自在东西方创造了辉煌灿烂的古老文明。在文明的发展进程之中，所有民族彼此互惠，对置身其中的世界，负有共同的责任，保护人类命运共同体。

　　值此展览开幕之际，我谨代表中华世纪坛艺术馆对意大利驻华大使馆、中国文物交流中心、意大利那不勒斯国家考古博物馆表示衷心的感谢。并借此机会向所有为推动中意两国文化交流做出贡献的朋友们表示衷心的感谢！感谢为展览付出辛劳的中意双方的同仁们。

　　祝展览圆满成功！

冀鹏程

中华世纪坛艺术馆馆长

Speech

China and Italy, located at both ends of the ancient Silk Road, share a history of over two-millennia of cultural exchange and interaction. In the new era, these two countries continue to serve as significant strategic partners to one another. Since its establishment in 2001, the China World Art Museum has fostered long-term cooperations with the museums as well as the arts and cultural industries in Italy, and has successively hosted a great number of exhibitions, such as *The Dawn of Rome: Etruscan Civilization in Italy, Italian Renaissance Art Exhibition* inaugurating the 2006 Italian Culture Year, *Tales from An Eruption: Pompeii, Herculaneum, Oplontis, Qin-Han and Roman Civilizations*, and *BOLDINI--MASTER OF THE BELLE EPOQUE*.

In early 2017, as one of the first members of the "China-Italy Cultural Cooperation Mechanism" established by the Chinese and Italian governments, the China World Art Museum opened a new chapter in Sino-Italian cultural exchanges. We have since organized a series of projects such as *PAESTUM, A City of the Ancient Mediterranean* and *WUJI: The Infinite Universe of Masterpieces from the Galleria Nazionale d'ArteModerna e Contemporanea*.

As one of the premier archaeological museums in the world, the National Archaeological Museum of Naples (MANN) has the world's most complete collection of ancient Roman sculptures and Pompeian frescoes. *The Light of Ancient Roman Civilization: Masterpieces From the National Archaeological Museum of Naples*, hosted by the China World Art Museum, will showcase their representative collection. The exhibition aims to not only explore the grandeur of human civilizations through the lens of art, but also trace the light of human wisdom and the source of spirit.

To engage with the world, we must first understand it. To stride into the future, we must comprehend our past. The exhibition focuses on the cultural exchange and mutual learning between Chinese and Western civilizations, takes "what is beauty" as the starting point, and gathers the treasures of the ancient Roman period. It presents Roman's classical beauty from different aspects and reveals the brilliant ancient Roman civilization to the public. Chinese audiences will be guided on a journey back to the epoch of ancient Rome and the Qin-Han dynasties, which enables them to comprehend and appreciate the artistic achievements of ancient Roman civilization.

Both China and Italy are nations with a profound history and have created splendid ancient civilizations. In the process of the development of civilization, all nations mutually benefit each other, bearing a shared responsibility towards the world in which we coexist, thereby safeguarding a community with a shared future for mankind.

On the occasion of the opening of this exhibition, on behalf of the China World Art Museum, I would like to express my heartfelt gratitude to the Italian Embassy in China, the China Cultural Heritage Exchange Center and the National Archaeological Museum of Naples. I seize this opportunity to express my sincere thanks to all the friends who have contributed to the promotion of cultural exchanges between China and Italy! Thank you to the colleagues from both sides who worked hard for the exhibition.

I wish the exhibition a complete success!

Ji Pengcheng
Director of China World Art Museum

致 辞

罗马与中国，鹰与龙，是两个古代世界中最为璀璨的伟大文明。这种璀璨的伟大，不仅源于他们的精锐之师，更在于文明内在的组织能力、基础建设水平和以万里长城及哈德良长城为代表的防御设施，以及对艺术、文学、哲学和崇高的执着追求与成就。

公元前1世纪末期，中国、罗马两大文明成为了东西方的焦点。绵延的商路穿过广袤无垠的草原，商贾和使节奔波于这条通路之间，绮丽珍贵的丝绸制品进入罗马境内，精致考究的陶器制品流入现在的北京地区，将鹰与龙的世界交织在一起。

回望这些呼应的历史现象，我们不难发现，这些古代文明的命运是从混乱中孕育秩序。在这种优渥的条件下，诗歌、文学、绘画、雕塑等各种艺术形式得以脱胎其中，人性的光辉投射在历史的间隙中。

在北京，紫禁城所在之地，那不勒斯国家考古博物馆通过本展览，提出了一个从罗马复杂社会中诞生的"美的宣言"——无论是在彼时还是当下，它也许不尽完美，也不尽公平，但却能攀登至令人惊叹的高度，甚至在工程领域超越了古希腊的成就。

那不勒斯国家考古博物馆几乎同当代的马可波罗一样，满怀喜悦地来到"天朝"，期望进一步加强两大文明千年以来的联系。我们由衷感谢中国政府的热情款待，与意大利驻华大使馆以及Mondo Mostre的精心组织。

洞察相似，理解差异，通过知识共同成长，是当今文化大国的核心价值体系。

保罗·朱利里尼
那不勒斯国家考古博物馆馆长

Speech

Rome and China, the Eagle and the Dragon, are undeniably the two greatest empires of the ancient world, not so much and not only for their armies, but for their organisational capacity, infrastructure, defensive systems (considering the Great Wall and Hadrian's Wall), arts, literature, philosophy, and concept of the sacred.

From the end of the 1st century B.C. onwards, the two kingdoms became the focal centres of the West and the East, while long caravan routes branching out across the steppes connected the two worlds, providing silk to Rome and ceramics to Beijing. Merchants and official delegations travelled along these routes.

According to some legends, even Romans captured after the defeat at Carrhae were sold as mercenary slaves to the Chinese and, later on, the Huns threatened both sides on several occasions.

It is the destiny of empires to represent, in these symmetries, order against disorder, to create the conditions for the best expressions of humanity to be manifested in poetry, literature, painting, sculpture.

What MANN proposes today in Beijing, the location of the Forbidden City, is a 'declaration of beauty' born out of the complex Roman society: perhaps not perfect and fair, not even for those times, but capable of incredible heights, sometimes superior, at least in the field of engineering, to the creations of ancient mother Greece.

The Archaeological Museum of Naples is therefore delighted, almost as a modern Marco Polo, to strengthen those relationships that have united us for millennia, coming to the Celestial Empire and can only thank the Chinese Government for the welcome, the Italian Embassy in China and Mondo Mostre for the organisation.

Seizing similarities, marvelling at differences, growing together through knowledge are the values of today's new cultural empires.

Paolo Giulierini
Director of National Archaeological Museum of Naples

罗马——"帝国的艺术，艺术的帝国"

马里奥·格里马尔迪博士 策展人

引言

古罗马帝国和秦汉王朝的外交关系源于公元前2世纪左右丝绸之路的开通，丝绸之路从塔里木盆地延伸到叙利亚地区，横跨400公里。这种地缘上一东一西的遥远距离，从侧面表明了古罗马文明和中华文明之间的关系基本上是间接的。中国古籍曾详细记载了罗马的器物、习俗、政治体制和城市建筑，一些古罗马历史学家也曾记录过这两大文明间的联系。

在这段时间内，历史见证了古代世界中对东西方影响深远的两个文明的形成与巩固，缔造了一个横跨欧洲、北非至亚洲的文明系统。一方面，古罗马帝国尚武的民族特质奠定了稳固的社会与政治基础，效仿并继承了亚历山大大帝的庞大疆域；另一方面，以秦朝的建立作为序幕，拉开了长达四百余年汉朝的繁荣统治。

古罗马历史学家老普林尼认为，或许两个文明的第一次相遇是借助波斯商队，在塔里木盆地边缘的"石塔"完成了会面。公元97年，汉朝使节甘英抵达中亚，并决心前往罗马，但居住在当地的居民为他描述了一条相去甚远的路径，这也使得他不得不在中途折返。在公元166年，马可·奥勒留时期，罗马帝国的外交使节曾抵达中国。这些接触的产生，不仅涉及一些原材料（如丝绸和织物）的交流，同时也是一种图像、风尚和文化的交融。物质之上，在精神领域，"人是有限的神，神是无限的人"的概念在此时期的两大文明中颇得共鸣。

意大利那不勒斯国家考古博物馆保存了丰富的雕塑、织物、壁画和马赛克。对这些藏品的图像及其表现形式进行分析，可以让研究延展至时尚和习俗领域，这让我们得以再次打开古代丝绸之路的大门，重拾罗马世界中曾丢失的基本色彩。

近年来，那不勒斯国家考古博物馆大力推动"色彩还原计划"。随着这项研究的推进，现在我们可以看到，雕塑作品上曾经也附着鲜艳的颜色。借助对服饰、实用器具以及人物面部特征的色彩提取，研究人员获得了更丰富的考古学材料，继而从图像以及符号学方面进一步加深了对古罗马文明的认知。

因此，通过展览中的雕塑和最新的研究，我们可以重新发现两个古代伟大文明之间的联系与交流，脱离出原有的单色世界，去重启一个丰富多彩的万花筒般的古代世界。

帝国的艺术，艺术的帝国

随着时间的推移，古罗马的疆域不断扩大，不同民族和文化的人们逐步接触与融合，共同构筑了一套由语言（拉丁语）、法律（罗马法）、货币（塞斯特修斯）和度量衡构成的政治文化系统。这种"全球化"的融合很大程度上尊重了不同民族和族群的习惯与传统。

罗马帝国的崛起代表着新的图像语言的形成。第一种方式就是对亚历山大大帝时期已有的图像语言系统的再利用：在罗马征服和扩张的过程中，大量优秀的艺术品被引入罗马，成为古罗马艺术家们模仿和学习的对象（例如：《维纳斯的背影》，详见图录编号60）。这进一步催生了具有罗马帝国特色的第二种表现方式，其中以朱里亚·克劳迪王朝艺术品中的奥古斯都形象最为典型。

《奥古斯都像》

现实主义的肖像和理想的肖像

图像变革的第一种方式体现在人物肖像中。新式君主或军事统帅的图像表现方式与先前的描绘形式已彻底决裂。以亚历山大为例，他常常被描绘成年轻、无须、衣冠不整且带有神性怒容的样子（例如：《战利品前的胜利女神与国王》，详见图录编号3）。奥古斯都时代的肖像脱离了时间的束缚，因为它超越了时间（被描绘对象的真实年龄并不重要），也超越了场合（军事肖像和宗教肖像具有相同的创作理念）。

随着朝代的更迭，我们可以看到保罗·赞克（Zanker）所描述的那种"图像的力量"的变化，每个新的家族都将创造一种源于其特定历史和政治背景的图像，来组成新的语言。（例如：《德米特里一世头像》，详见图录编号15）

从伪塞涅卡（详见图录编号17）到赫耳墨斯，再到皇室成员的肖像，我们正踏上古罗马文明的图像之旅。

罗马人的颜色

在古罗马社会，绘画工作往往由贫民、奴隶、妇女以及其他无法参与政治军事事务的人完成。绘画艺术也大多与戏剧相关联。

公元79年维苏威火山爆发，赫库兰尼姆、庞贝和斯塔比亚等一众古罗马城市被火山灰掩埋，这使得它们成为保存最完整的考古学案例之一。通过重新构建，我们得以从空间的功能关系入手，研究空间和装饰的关系。事实上，目前对于它们的研究已经更多地融入对"风格"的类型学分析中去。在这种情况下，壁画上的画面将古罗马住宅中房屋功能、空间结构以及装饰之间相辅相成的关系浓缩在平面绘画之中，对于研究至关重要。

因此，这次展览提出阐述内容的视角就是在上述方法论下，重新解读那些被维苏威火山爆发所掩埋城市中的杰出壁画。这些藏品为我们提供了观察和感知多彩的古罗马社会的机会，并通过那些匿名的画师创作的图像，来感受久远艺术品传递出的微茫讯息与历史辉煌。

The Romans, "Men with Big Noses": An Art for the Empire, An Empire for the Art

Dr. Phd Mario Grimaldi Curator of the Exhibition

Introduction

Relations between the Roman Empire and the Chinese Empire were essentially indirect until the end of the two powers. Diplomatic relations began with the opening of the Silk Road around the 2nd century B.C. Contacts began around 130 BCE until the attempt to send a delegation to Rome around 100 CE. Based on ancient Chinese records, some Roman embassies also arrived in China: the first seems to date back to the Roman emperor Marcus Aurelius and arrived in the Far East in 166 CE. The Chinese chronicles report in great detail the Roman uses and customs, the system of government, the architecture of the city, but even the Roman historians testify to the existence of contact with that distant empire.

The first fundamental step for contacts was the opening of the Silk Road, which opened a bridge between the Far East and the West, following the expansion of the empire of Alexander the Great towards Central Asia up to the Valley of Fergana. The Silk Road stretched for 400 kilometers from Syria to the Tarim Basin with multiple trading posts where the first trade contacts took place. Rome did not have direct contacts with China, since the goods did not travel on a single route, but passed from caravan to caravan. The meeting point between the merchants of Persia and the Chinese merchants is identified by Pliny the Elder in the Stone Tower which stood on the edge of the Tarim.

Between the 3rd and 2nd century BCE, we are witnessing on a planetary level the formation and consolidation of the two largest and longest-lived empires of the ancient world from West to East, two empires that will range from Europe to North Africa to Asia. If, on the one hand, Rome in this period laid the social and political foundations of its radical presence in Italy and its conquest of the seas, effectively inheriting the great Kingdom of Alexander the Great in the Middle East, on the other hand, the foundation of the kingdom of the Qin, which lasted only 15 years, from 221 to 209 BCE, represents the prelude to the Han rule, whose dynasty reigned from 206 BCE to 220 CE.

Thus there was an intensification of trade along the Silk Road where goods began to circulate from Europe to India and China. Mutual embassy trips to Parthia and Syria began, in order to strengthen control over goods. The Parthian Kingdom was the kingpin of these two great cultural and social as well as economic and military powers.

The Parthians had always had a policy aimed at not creating a direct relationship between the two economic superpowers, in this way they ensured the profitable role of intermediaries.

At the end of the 1st century BCE, some Roman prisoners arrived in China after being taken as such by the Huns and were settled by the Chinese in the province of Gansu in a city which took the name of Li-Jien (Da Qin). A few years later (9 CE) Emperor Wang renamed the city to Jieh-lu (Raised Prisoners).

When Gan Ying, Chinese ambassador and military man, in 97 CE, he arrived in central Asia, determined to arrive in Rome as he had been ordered, the peoples who inhabited these areas described him a different itinerary to reach Italy, much longer than in reality, and forced him to go back.

The birth of these contacts involved an exchange not only of raw materials such as silk and fabrics but was also a vehicle for iconographies, repertoires of images as well as fashions, habits and customs.

Silk was the main product requested and sought after by the Romans. The thread obtained from the *larvae* of *lepidoptera* and the ability to work it into fabrics also allowed the possibility of conveying images and myths, creating an iconographic exchange between West and East. The exchanges, however, did not only concern the precious fabric but also other products, such as jade and lacquers.

The philosophical concept of the type "*man is a mortal God, God an immortal man*" is the most similar between the two peoples since at least the imperial age.

The two empires of the Ta-Ch' in (Romans in the Chinese sources) and the Syrians (Chinese in the Latin ones) were enclosed and protected by the Walls of Romulus on one side and by the Great Wall on the other but their economic foresight contributed to an exchange of ideas, fashions and materials that we can find today in the analysis and comparison of the sculptural and chromatic repertoires that have come down to us.

These aspects briefly stated in this introduction find confirmation in the beautiful sculptural, textile, decorative specimens (frescoes and mosaics) preserved in the National Archaeological Museum of Naples which are part of the various collections preserved there (Farnese, Excavations of Herculaneum and Pompeii) and exhibited here. Through the analysis of the iconographic representation fashions of these works it is possible to reopen the ancient Silk Road again, even if only in an ideal way, through the analysis of the fashions and customs but above all recovering the fundamental element of color apparently lost in the Roman world (with the exception of the decoration of the rooms of the houses).

Contrary to what was conventionally believed at least until 13 years ago, the ancient Western world is a world that speaks through colors which have the task of distinguishing ethnic origins, materials and social statuses.

In recent years, the National Archaeological Museum has promoted an intense program of recovery of the color still present on the fantastic sculptural repertoire preserved in it.

Through technical-scientific analysis it is possible to document the presence of different colors present on the exposed statues. We pass from the color of the clothes of the gods to those of the emperors up to the saddles of the horses.

Even the faces of the individual characters were characterized by color to define their origin, the gods generally blond (with golden hair), the emperors with their strong and decisive physiognomic characters (in the definition, for example, of the transition from the Giulio Claudia fashion of representation without beard to Antonina with beard, an element that greatly affected the Chinese iconographic imagination).

Through the sculptural specimens present in the exhibition, it will thus be possible to recover a world of contacts and exchanges between two great superpowers of the ancient world, starting from an apparent state of monochrome to then recover a kaleidoscopic world of colors and materials typical of these two great societies.

An art for the empire, an empire for the art

The circular vision of the exhibition plans to bring the visitor into the social world that characterizes the other largest empire in history together with the Chinese one.

The widening of the territorial boundaries of Rome's power entails a gradual process of contact over time between different peoples and peoples in every socio-cultural form. Different and distant populations for traditions and customs gradually find themselves having an all-intelligible reference language, Latin, a set of laws to refer to, Roman law, a single currency, the sestertius, a system of weights and measures to refer to. However, this first protoform of globalization takes into great account the habits and customs of different peoples and different ethnic groups.

With the birth of the empire of Rome, understood as a command, the need also arises for the Urbe itself to carry out a change in the language of images to be understood and accepted by as many people as possible. This occurs in two ways which will be explained in this first section with the help of the pieces on display. The first is linked to the reuse of the intercultural language already created with Alexander the Great throughout the Middle East; with the victory of Rome over Greece and over the last descendant of Alexander we begin to have the arrival of great works of art in the city (see object #60: *Venus Callipige*) created by those great masters such as Lysippos, Praxiteles etc. that show a new way of representing themselves. This leads to the second way of communicating on the part of the new course of the Empire especially with the Julio-Claudian dynasty and with the figure of Augustus who is the first to be the only true catalyst of different forces between the Senate and the People (now ranging from the Pillars of Hercules to the realm of Central Asian peoples).

Augusto creates a new form of universal language made of images with a strong iconographic and iconological value but above all understandable by everyone! A new language of power through the image pervades the whole Mediterranean.

The realistic portrait and the ideal one

The first form of change in the communication of images is recorded in portraits. As already happened with Alexander the Great who, with his being portrayed young, beardless, disheveled and with a look of divine fury, marked a clear break between the way of being represented by the great western kings or generals and his new course, so too Augustus marked a watershed bringing the Roman veristic portrait towards a new ideal path beyond time and occasions. In fact, the portrait in the Augustan age is out of time because it is beyond time (the realistic age of the subject represented does not matter) and it is also out of occasion (the face for a military portrait has the same ideal concept as the one made

for a sacred occasion).

With the change of dynasties, we are witnessing a change in the "power of images" as described by Zanker, each new family will create a new language made of images specific to its history and its politics. (see object #15: *Head of Demetrio Poliercete*)

The portraits and herms featured in this section from the Pseudo Seneca (see object #17) up to the imperial ones will take us on this journey of images of the "*men with big noses*".

The colors of Romans

In Roman society, therefore, which in any case recognized the art of painting in its origins "*Even among the Romans, painting was honored very soon, since a famous gens of the Fabi derived the surname of Painters from this art; and the first who bore this surname painted the Tempio della Salute with his own hand...*" (Pliny the Elder, NH, XXXV, 195), this original relationship between painting and patrician high society then deteriorated, bringing back the art manifestation of painting at the lowest margins of the community, relegating it as the work of freedmen, slaves, women and people incapable of political and military life, linked more to the world of theater (fig.1).

Fig.1 Painter with painted statue and framed painting from a fresco in Pompeii

Fig.2 Fresco, *Hercules and Omphale* (partially)

The case of the cities buried by the Vesuvian eruption of 79 CE, Herculaneum, Pompeii and Stabia, appears to be one of the most complete for the exceptional contextualization of the decorative elements which, perfectly preserved in situ, thus allow to recompose those spatial-functional relationships of the context, decorative giving us the possibility to keep faith methodologically to the concept of the relationship between space and decoration and above all of context. In fact, the interest in the relationships between the decoration of the rooms and their function has increasingly been integrated into the typological analysis of the "styles". In this context, the figure of the picture appears to be fundamental for translating into images the existing and necessary relationship for the client between space, his house, and decoration.

The experience proposed with this exhibition is therefore to re-read, within this methodological perspective, some great decorative examples belonging to the Fresco Collection of the National Archaeological Museum of Naples from those cities that were buried by the great eruption of Vesuvius in 79 CE still offer us the opportunity to investigate and be part of that splendid deception through the personality of the *pictores* who operated anonymously in those houses.

The recognition of the painters who worked in individual houses can also make use of unique reference models found in the compositions of the figures represented, which however always betray the personality of the individual artist. The existence of models to be used and consulted at the time of the realization of the decorative works by the *redemptor*, that is the one who organized the work of the artisans-painters, is attested both on an iconographic basis (fig.2), and material as well as being quoted in the sources: "*Of him (Xenokrates ed.) there remain many drawings and sketches in pencil on boards and papyri, from which it is said that artists profit.*" (Pliny the Elder, NH, XXXV, 68).

Then the arrival of original Greek works in Rome and in almost all the cities of Italy starting from the 2nd century BCE., contributed to the creation of a certainly more varied iconographic language.

The serial reproduction of many of these works is easily understood from the technical analysis possible here of several examples with identical subjects reinterpreted by different painters, such as the example of the Three Graces, of which there was certainly an original model made by an artist of the Hellenistic age, we do not know whether sculptor or painter, which the sources are silent, but who has had great fortune throughout the history of art through the illustrious replicas of artists such as Botticelli, Raphael, Canova, and Picasso to name a few.

Alongside the Hellenistic models there were also new iconographies peculiar to Roman language, history and society. This is the case, for example, of the story in images of the codification of the feeling of pietas with Micon and Pero which became an example of behavior, with a strong and natural evocative impact, to be recovered and enhanced not only in Rome with the construction of the Pietas Temple, as told by Valerio Massimo, but also in cities like Pompeii where there are several examples of which one is still in situ, the House of Marco Lucretius Frontone in Pompeii, completed by the motto praising the pietas and by the names of the characters represented: "*Those foods that the mother offered to the little ones born unjust fate turned into food for the father. The gesture is worthy of eternity. Look: on the gaunt neck the senile veins are already pulsing with the flowing milk while Pero herself approaches her face and caresses Micone. There is a sad modesty mixed with pity.*" (CIL IV, 6635c).

This story in images also became part of the historical and artistic repertoire of many illustrious successors called to replicate this theme in different spatial contexts, both in Roman and later times, as for example Caravaggio did in his admirable synthesis work for the Pio Monte della Misericordia of Naples, the Seven Works of Mercy.

Technically, the realization and reproduction of many of these themes on different supports and with different measures was possible thanks to the use of precise reference schemes achievable through the use of grids for the overall decorative schemes and *sinopiae* for the figures that thus the reproduction of the same subject in different scales.

These technical solutions were not only used for the frescoed walls but also for the realization of the mosaics in a possible exchange of images that had no limits of support, size and time if you think of the wonderful mosaics of the Villa in Piazza Armerina.

An example of how this could happen comes from what is visible below the mosaic with polychrome tesserae and meander motif with perspective cubes, found in the excavations of the garden of the House of Marco Fabio Rufo, where the orthogonal grid visible in the engraved sinopia is preserved and painted. The preparation was carried out after smoothing the last layer of the preparation cocciopesto, on which a regular grid formed by squares and rectangles was engraved, useful for reproducing the original drawing in scale; bands of color were spread inside the grid to indicate the chromatic choice and the number of lines of the tiles.

The overall picture that is outlined in our eyes is that of a much more dynamic and differentiated ancient world in which the figure of the painter lived a social condition of public anonymity yet to be understood from many points of view.

The destiny of these men who decorated and embellished the houses of all citizen of Rome and the cities connected to it, starting at least from the middle of the 1st century BCE, was to remain without identity in an artistic anonymity that today we try to recognize, understand and attribute.

Bibliografia

Adamo Muscettola 1983   Adamo Muscettola S., Un nuovo Alessandro da Pompei e gli aspetti della "imitatio Alexandri" augustea, in RendAccNap, 58, Napoli 1983, pp. 275-295.

Adamo Muscettola 1990   Adamo Muscettola S., Il ritratto di Lucio Calpurnio Pisone Pontefice da Ercolano, in CronErc, 20, pp. 145-156.

Allroggen-Bedel 1991   Allroggen-Bedel A., Lokalstile in der campanischen Wandmalerei, in KölnJb, 24, pp. 35-42.

Allroggen-Bedel 2002   Allroggen-Bedel A., Gli scavi borbonici nelle ville stabiane: pitture antiche e gusto settecentesco, in Bonifacio G., Sodo A.M. (a cura di), Stabiae: Storia ed Architettura, Roma 2002, pp. 101-107.

Anderson 1987   Anderson M.L., The Portrait Medaillons of the Imperial Villa at Boscotrecase, in AJA 91, 1987.

Andreae 1977   Andreae B., Das Alexandermosaik aus Pompeji: mit einem Vorwort des Verlegers und einem Anhang: Goethes Interpretation des Alexandermosaiks, Recklinghausen 1977.

Andronikos 1984   Andronikos M., Vergina. The Royal tombs, Athens 1984.

Baldassarre, et alii 2002   Baldassarre I., Pontrandolfo A., Rouveret A., Salvadori M., Pittura romana. Dall'ellenismo al tardo-antico, Milano 2002.

Balty 1978   Balty J.C., La statue de bronze de Titus Quintius Flamininus, in MEFRA, 90, pp. 669-686.

Barbet 2000   Barbet A., La pittura romana, dal pictor al restauratore, Imola 2000.

Barbet, Verbanck-Piérard 2013   Barbet A., Verbanck-Piérard A. (a cura di), La villa romaine de Boscoreale et ses fresques, Arles 2013.

Bergmann 2010   Bergmann B., New perspectives on the Villa of Publius Fannius Synistor at Boscoreale, in Bergmann B., De Caro S.,

MERTENS J.R., MEYER R., ROMAN FRESCOES FROM BOSCOREALE, THE METROPOLITAN OF ART, NEW YORK 2010, PP. 11-32.

BIANCHI BANDINELLI 1965 BIANCHI BANDINELLI R., S.V. RITRATTO, IN EAA VOL. VI, 1965, PP. 695-738.

BIANCHI BANDINELLI 1973 BIANCHI BANDINELLI R., STORICITÀ DELL'ARTE CLASSICA, BARI 1973.

BIANCHI BANDINELLI 1980 BIANCHI BANDINELLI R., LA PITTURA ANTICA, ROMA 1980.

BIEBER 1973 BIEBER M., THE DEVELOPMENT OF PORTRAITURE ON ROMAN REPUBLICAN COINS, IN ANRW 1, 4, BERLIN 1973, PP. 871-898.

BONACASA-RIZZA 1988 BONACASA N., RIZZA G., (A CURA DI), RITRATTO UFFICIALE E RITRATTO PRIVATO. ATTI II CONF. INTERN. RITRATTO ROMANO (= QUADERNI RICERCA SCIENTIFICA, CNR N° 116) ROMA 1988.

BRAGANTINI 1997 BRAGANTINI I. VII, 16 (INS. OCC.), 22. CASA DI M. FABIUS RUFUS , IN: PPM VII, ROMA 1997, PP. 947-1125

BRAGANTINI 2004 BRAGANTINI I., UNA PITTURA SENZA MAESTRI: LA PRODUZIONE DELLA PITTURA PARIETALE ROMANA, JRA 17, 2004, PP. 131-145.

BRAGANTINI 2007 BRAGANTINI I., LA PITTURA IN ETÀ TARDOREPUBBLICANA, IN ZEVI F. ET ALII (A CURA DI), VILLAS, MAISONS, SANCTUAIRES ET TOMBEAUX TARDO-RÉPUBLICAINS: DÉCOUVERTES ET RELECTURES RÉCENTES, ROMA 2007, PP. 123-132.

BRAGANTINI, SAMPAOLO 2009 BRAGANTINI I., SAMPAOLO V., LA PITTURA POMPEIANA, MILANO 2009.

BRECKENRIDGE 1973 BRECKENRIDGE J.D., ORIGINS OF ROMAN REPUBLICAN PORTRAITURE: RELATIONS WITH THE HELLENISTIC WORLD, IN ANRW 1, 4, BERLIN 1973, PP. 826- 854.

CANFORA 2011 CANFORA L., LA MERAVIGLIOSA STORIA DEL FALSO ARTEMIDORO, PALERMO 2011.

CARLIER, 1984 CARLIER P., LA ROYAUTÉ EN GRÈCE AVANT ALEXANDRE, STRASBOURG 1984.

CELANI 1998 CELANI A., OPERE D'ARTE GRECHE NELLA ROMA DI AUGUSTO, PERUGIA 1998.

CELANI 2013 CELANI A., UNA CERTA INQUIETUDINE NATURALE: SCULTURE ELLENISTICHE FRA SENSO E SIGNIFICATO, PERUGIA 2013.

CIARDIELLO 2003 CIARDIELLO R., LE ANTICHITÀ DI ERCOLANO ESPOSTE, IN PALMIERI S. (A CURA DI), SAGGI PER MARCELLO GIGANTE, NAPOLI 2003, PP. 435-448.

CIARDIELLO 2006 CIARDIELLO R., VI 17 INSULA OCCIDENTALIS 42. CASA DEL BRACCIALE D'ORO, IN M. AOYAGI, U. PAPPALARDO (A CURA DI), POMPEI. (REGIONES VI- VII). INSULA OCCIDENTALIS, NAPOLI 2006, PP. 69-256.

CIARDIELLO 2012 CIARDIELLO R., ALCUNE RIFLESSIONI SULLA CASA DEL BRACCIALE D'ORO A POMPEI, IN: ANNALI DELL'UNIVERSITÀ DEGLI STUDI SUOR ORSOLA BENIN- CASA, 2011-2012. ARCHEOLOGIA. STUDI E RICERCHE SUL CAMPO, NAPOLI 2012, PP. 167-193.

COARELLI 1995 COARELLI F., DA PERGAMO A ROMA. I GALATI NELLA CITTÀ DEGLI ATTALIDI, ROMA 1995.

COARELLI 1996 COARELLI F., REVIXIT ARS, ROMA 1996.

COARELLI 2010 COARELLI F., NAVALIA POMPEIANA, IN C. GASPARRI, R. GRECO, R. PIEROBON (A CURA DI), DALLA STORIA ALL'IMMAGINE, INCONTRO DI STUDI PER RICORDARE STEFANIA ADAMO MUSCETTOLA, NAPOLI 2010, PP. 451-457.

COARELLI 2014 COARELLI, F. (A CURA DI), LA GLORIA DEI VINTI. PERGAMO, ATENE, ROMA. CATALOGO DELLA MOSTRA (ROMA, 18 APRILE - 7 SETTEMBRE 2014), MILANO 2014.

D'AMBROSIO-DE CARO 1983 D'AMBROSIO A., DE CARO S., UN IMPEGNO PER POMPEI. LA NECROPOLI DI PORTA NOCERA, MILANO 1983.

DE FRANCISCIS 1939 DE FRANCISCIS A., RITRATTI ROMANI NEL MUSEO NAZIONALE DI NAPOLI, MEMNAPOLI 6, PP. 201-224.

DE CARO 1994 DE CARO S. (A CURA DI), IL MUSEO ARCHEOLOGICO NAZIONALE DI NAPOLI, NAPOLI 1994.

DE CAROLIS 2007 DE CAROLIS E. ET ALII, UN CONTRIBUTO SULLA TECNICA DI ESECUZIONE DEGLI AFFRESCHI DELLA VILLA DEI PAPIRI DI ERCOLANO, IN AUTOMATA 2, 2007.

DE CAROLIS 2012 DE CAROLIS E. ET ALII, RIFLESSIONI SUL QUADRO DELLA VENERE IN CONCHIGLIA DI POMPEI: DAL MITO AL LAVORO DEI PICTORES, IN RIVISTA DI STU- DI POMPEIANI 23, 2012.

DE FRANCISCIS 1951 DE FRANCISCIS A., IL RITRATTO ROMANO A POMPEI, MEMNAPOLI VOL. 1, NAPOLI 1951.

DE VOS 1981 DE VOS M., LA BOTTEGA DEI PITTORI DI VIA CASTRICIO, IN POMPEI 1748-1980. I TEMPI DELLA DOCUMENTAZIONE (MOSTRA, ROMA-POMPEI, LUGLIO- OTTOBRE 1981), ROMA 1981, PP. 119-130.

DRERUP 1980 DRERUP H., TOTENMASKE UND AHNENBILD BEI DEN RÖMERN, RÖMMITT 87, PP. 81SS. (SOTTOLINEA GLI ASPETTI MAGICI DELLA MASCHERA FUNERARIA).

ELIA 1938 ELIA O., ICONOGRAFIA AULICA ROMANA IN PITTURE STABIANE, BOLLARTE 23, PP. 101-114.

EHRARDT 2009 EHRARDT W., DAS ALEXANDERMOSAIK ODER : WIE AUTHENTISCH MUSSEINE HISTORISCHE DARSTELLUNG SEIN?, IN MITTEILUNGEN DES DEUTSCHEN AR- CHÄOLOGISCHEN INSTITUTS, RÖMISCHE ABTEILUNG, 114.2008, 2009, PP. 215-269.

ESPOSITO 2009A ESPOSITO D., LE OFFICINE PITTORICHE DI IV STILE A POMPEI. DINAMICHE PRODUTTIVE ED ECONOMICO-SOCIALI, ROMA 2009.

ESPOSITO 2009B ESPOSITO D., FILOSSENO, IL CICLOPE E SESTO POMPEO. PROGRAMMI FIGURATIVI E >PROPAGANDA< POLITICA NELLE DOMUS

DELL'ARISTOCRAZIA POMPEIANA DELLA TARDA ETÀ REPUBBLICANA, IN JAHRBUCH DES DEUTSCHEN ARCHÄOLOGISCHEN INSTITUTS, BAND 123.2008, 2009.

ESPOSITO 2014 — ESPOSITO D., LA PITTURA DI ERCOLANO, ROMA 2014.

ESPOSITO-FALCUCCI-FERRARA 2011 — ESPOSITO F., FALCUCCI C., FERRARA D., LA TECNICA ESECUTIVA DEI DIPINTI DEL SALONE 5 DELLA VILLA DEI MISTERI: CENTO ANNI DI IPOTESI E RI- CERCHE, IN RIVISTA DI STUDI POMPEIANI 22, 2011.

FITTSCHEN 1975 — FITTSCHEN K., ZUM FIGURENFRIES DER VILLA VON BOSCOREALE, IN B. ANDRAE-H. KYRIELEIS (A CURA DI), NEUE FORSCHUNGEN IN POMPEJI, RECK- LINGHAUSEN 1975, PP. 93-100.

FITTSCHEN 1985 — FITTSCHEN K., SUL RUOLO DEL RITRATTO ANTICO NELL'ARTE ITALIANA, IN: S. SETTIS (A CURA DI), MEMORIA DELL'ANTICO, VOL. 2, TORINO 1985, PP. 381-412.

FUCHS 1998 — FUCHS M., AURA AETAS: EIN GLÜCKVERHEISSENDES SIBYLLINUM IM GROSSEN OECUS DER VILLA VON BOSCOREALE, IN JAHRBUCH DES DEUTSCHEN AR- CHÄOLOGISCHEN INSTITUTS, BAND 113, BERLIN 1998, PP. 91-108.

GASPARRI 1994 — GASPARRI C., COPIE E COPISTI, IN ENCICLOPEDIA DELL'ARTE ANTICA, VOL. II, 1994, P. 804.

GIULIANI 1990 — GIULIANI L., ZUR SPÄTREPUBLIKANISCHEN BILDNISKUNST. WEGE UND ABWEGE DER INTERPRETATION ANTIKER PORTRÄTS, ANTABENDL 36, 1990, PP. 103- 115.

GIULIANI 1991 — GIULIANI L., BILDNIS UND BOTSCHAFT. HERMENEUTISCHE UNTERSUCHUNG ZUR BILDNISKUNST DER RÖMISCHEN REPUBLIK, FRANKFURT (SURKAMP) 1986 (RECENS.: K. FITTSCHEN, "PATHOSSTEIGERUNG UND PATHOSDÄMP- FUNG. BEMERKUNGEN ZU GRIECHISCHEN UND RÖMISCHEN PORTRÄTS DES 2. UND 1. JHS V. CHR., ARCHANZ, 1991, PP. 253-270).

GOMBRICH 1999 — GOMBRICH E., LA STORIA DELL'ARTE, HONG KONG 1999.

GÖTZ LAHUSEN 1984 — GÖTZ LAHUSEN, SCHRIFTQUELLEN ZUM RÖMISCHEN BILDNIS. TEXTSTELLEN VON DEN ANFÄNGEN BIS ZUM 3. JHD. N. CHR., BREMEN (HEYE) RACCOLTA COMPLETA DELLE FONTI, 1984.

GÖTZ LAHUSEN 1985 — GÖTZ LAHUSEN, ZUR FUNKTION UND REZEPTION DES RÖMISCHEN AHNENBILDES, RÖMMITT 92, 1985, PP. 261-289, TAVV. 106-115.

GÖTZ LAHUSEN 1989 — GÖTZ LAHUSEN, DIE BILDNISMÜNZEN DER RÖMISCHEN REPUBLIK, MÜNCHEN (HIRMER) 1989.

GRIMALDI 2006 — GRIMALDI M., VII 16 INSULA OCCIDENTALIS 22. CASA DI M. FABIUS RUFUS, IN M. AOYAGI, U. PAPPALARDO (A CURA DI), POMPEI. (REGIONES VI- VII). INSULA OCCIDENTALIS, NAPOLI 2006, PP. 257-418.

GRIMALDI 2007A — GRIMALDI M., L'ICONOGRAFIA DI ALESSANDRO MAGNO A POMPEI, IN C. G. PELEGRIN (A CURA DI), CIRCULACION DE TEMAS Y SISTEMAS DECORATIVOS EN LA PINTURA MURAL ANTIGUA, AIPMA 2004, ZARAGOZA, PP. 331- 333.

GRIMALDI 2007B — GRIMALDI M., LA FASE REPUBBLICANA DELLA CASA DI MARCO FABIO RUFO A POMPEI, IN J.P. MORET (A CURA DI), VILLAS, MAISONS, SANCTUAI- RES ET TOMBEAUX TARDO-RÉPUBLICAINS: DECOUVERTES ET RELECTURES RE- CENTES: ATTI DEL CONVEGNO INTERNAZIONALE SULLA PITTURA DI II STILE IN ETÀ TARDO REPUBBLICANA, ROMA 2007, PP. 133-155.

GRIMALDI 2007C — GRIMALDI M., LA FASE REPUBBLICANA DELLA VILLA DI ARIANNA A STABIA, IN J.P. MORET (A CURA DI), VILLAS, MAISONS, SANCTUAIRES ET TOMBEAUX TARDO-RÉPUBLICAINS: DECOUVERTES ET RELECTURES RECENTES: ATTI DEL CON- VEGNO INTERNAZIONALE SULLA PITTURA DI II STILE IN ETÀ TARDO REPUBBLI- CANA, ROMA 2007, PP. 177-194.

GRIMALDI 2009 — GRIMALDI M., LA CASA DI MARCO FABIO RUFO A POMPEI, IN: CORALINI A. (A CURA DI), VESUVIANA ARCHEOLOGIE A CONFRONTO, CONVEGNO INTERNAZIONALE, (BOLOGNA 14-16 GENNAIO 2008), CITTÀ DI CASTELLO 2009, PP. 447-462.

GRIMALDI 2011 — GRIMALDI M., ALCUNI ESEMPI DI RIFLESSI DELLA GRANDE SCULTURA ELLENISTICA NELLA PITTURA ROMANO-CAMPANA, IN G.F. LA TORRE E M. TORELLI (A CURA DI), ATTI DEL CONVEGNO "LINGUAGGI E TRADIZIONI DELLA PITTURA ELLENISTICA IN ITALIA E IN SICILIA" (2009), ROMA 2011, PP. 547-560.

GRIMALDI 2013 — GRIMALDI M., LA VILLA DE PUBLIUS FANNIUS SYNISTOR ET LE PAGUS FELIX SUBURBANUS, IN BARBET A., VERBANCK-PIÉRARD A. (A CURA DI), LA VILLA ROMAINE DE BOSCOREALE ET SES FRESQUES, II, ARLES 2013, PP. 65- 78.

GRIMALDI 2014 — GRIMALDI M. (A CURA DI), LA CASA DI MARCO FABIO RUFO: NUOVI STUDI E RICERCHE, NAPOLI 2014.

GUIDOBALDI 2008 — GUIDOBALDI M. P. (A CURA DI), ERCOLANO. TRE SECOLI DI SCOPERTE, (NAPOLI MUSEO ARCHEOLOGICO NAZIONALE 16 OTTOBRE 2008-13 APRILE 2009), MILANO 2008.

GUIDOBALDI-ESPOSITO 2012 — GUIDOBALDI M.P., ESPOSITO D., ERCOLANO, COLORI DA UNA CITTÀ SEPOLTA, VERONA 2012.

HAUSER 2001 — HAUSER A., STORIA SOCIALE DELL'ARTE, VOL. I, TORINO 2001.

HIESINGER 1973 — HIESINGER U.W., PORTRAITURE IN THE ROMAN REPUBLIC, ANRW 1, 4, BERLIN 1973, PP. 805-825.

KASCHNITZ WEINBERG 1954 — KASCHNITZ WEINBERG G., BILDNISSE FRIEDRICHS II. VON HOHENSTAUFEN, RÖMMITT 60/61, 1954, PP. 1-21, TAVV. 1-13 (ESTRATTO).

LAGI DE CARO 1988 — LAGI DE CARO A., ALESSANDRO E ROSSANE COME ARES E AFRODITE IN UN DIPINTO DELLA CASA REGIO VI, INSULA

OCCIDENTALIS, N. 42, IN: STUDIA POMPEIANA ET CLASSICA IN HONOR OF WILHELMINA JASHEMSKI, NEW YORK 1988, PP. 75-88.

LEHMANN 1953   LEHMANN P.W., ROMAN WALL-PAINTINGS FROM BOSCOREALE IN THE METROPOLITAN MUSEUM OF ART, CAMBRIDGE MASS. 1953.

LING 1990   LING R., LA CASA DEL MENANDRO, IN: PPM II, ROMA 1990, PP. 240-397.

LING 1997   LING R., THE INSULA OF MENANDER AT POMPEII. THE STRUCTURES, OXFORD 1997.

LING 2003   LING R., LA CASA DEL MENANDRO, IN: STEFANI G. (A CURA DI), MENANDER. LA CASA DEL MENANDRO DI POMPEI, MILANO 2003, PP. 10-45.

MAFFEI 1994   MAFFEI S. (A CURA DI), LUCIANO DI SAMOSATA. DESCRIZIONE DI OPERE D'ARTE, TORINO 1994.

MAIURI 1932   MAIURI A., LA CASA DEL MENANDRO E IL SUO TESORO DI ARGENTERIA, ROMA 1932.

MAIURI1940   MAIURI A., PICTURAE LIGNEIS FORMIS INCLUSAE. NOTE SULLA TECNICA DELLA PITTURA CAMPANA, ESTRATTO DAL FASC. 7-9, SERIE VII, VOL. I, 1940.

MELILLO 2012   MELILLO L., "IL GRAN MUSAICO POMPEIANO DELLA CASA DEL FAUNO DI POMPEI. LE VICENDE CONSERVATIVE, GLI INTRIGHI DI CORTE, IL TRASFERIMENTO PRESSO IL REAL MUSEO DI NAPOLI, LA COLLOCAZIONE DEFINITIVA.", IN G. GAMBARDELLA, (A CURA DI), "ATLANTE DI POMPEI.", N. 35, NAPOLI 2012, PP. 81-94.

MEYBOOM 1979   MEYBOOM P.G.P., A MOSAIC PORTRAIT AT DELOS, BABESCH 54, PP. 111-114, FIGG. 1-2.

MOORMANN 1988   MOORMANN E.M., LA PITTURA PARIETALE ROMANA COME FONTE DI CONOSCENZA PER LA SCULTURA ANTICA, ASSEN 1988.

MOORMANN-PETERS 1995   MOORMANN E.M., PETERS W.J.T., I PITTORI DELLA CASA DI MARCUS LUCRETIUS FRONTO A POMPEI. RIFLESSIONI UN ANNO DOPO, IN MEDEDROM 54, 1995, PP. 214-227.

MOORMANN 2008   MOORMANN E.M., STATUES ON THE WALL : THE REPRESENTATION OF STATUARY IN ROMAN WALL PAINTING, IN THE SCULPTURAL ENVIRONMENT OF THE ROMAN NEAR EAST REFLECTIONS ON CULTURE, IDEOLOGY, AND POWER PP. 197- 224.

MORELLI 1890   MORELLI G., STUDI DI CRITICA D'ARTE SULLA PITTURA ITALIANA, 1890.

MORENO 1994   MORENO P., LA CITTÀ MUSEO: DISTRIBUZIONE DELLE OPERE DI LISPPO A ROMA DALL'ETÀ REPUBBLICANA ALLA TARDA ANTICHITÀ, IN LA CIUDAD EN EL MUNDO ROMANO. XIV CONGRESSO INTERNATIONAL DE ARQUEOLOGIA CLA- SICA (ATTI CONGRESSO TARRAGONA 1993), TARRAGONA 1994, II, P. 297.

MORENO 1995   MORENO P., ALESSANDRO E GLI ARTISTI DEL SUO TEMPO, IN: ALESSANDRO MAGNO. STORIA E MITO (CATALOGO DELLA MOSTRA, PALAZZO RUSPOLI) , RO- MA 1995.

MORENO 2000   MORENO P., APELLE. LA BATTAGLIA DI ALESSANDRO, MILANO 2000.

MORENO 2004   MORENO P., ALESSANDRO MAGNO. IMMAGINI COME STORIA, ROMA 2004.

MORENO 2007   MORENO P., POETI A POMPEI, ARCHEO 266, APRILE 2007, PP. 116-119.

MORET-PELLETIER-ZEVI 2007   MORET J.M., PELLETIER A., ZEVI F., VILLAS, MAISONS, SANCTUAIRES ET TOMBEAUX TARDO-RÉPUBLICAINS: DÉCOUVERTES ET RELECTURES RÉCENTES: AC- TES DU COLLOQUE INTERNATIONAL DE SAINT-ROMAIN-EN-GAL EN L'HONNEUR D'ANNA GALLINA ZEVI : VIENNE, SAINT-ROMAIN-EN-GAL, 8-10 FÉVRIER 2007 / COLLOQUE ORGANISÉ PAR FAUSTO ZEVI, JEAN MARC MORET ET AN- DRÉ PELLETIER ; TEXTES RASSEMBLÉS ET ÉDITÉS PAR BERTRAND PERRIER, ROMA 2007.

PAPPALARDO 1982   PAPPALARDO U., IL FREGIO CON EROTI FRA GIRALI NELLA SALA DEI MISTERI A POMPEI, IN JAHRBUCH DES DEUTSCHEN ARCHÄOLOGISCHEN INSTITUTS 97 1982, PP. 251-280.

PAPPALARDO 1991   PAPPALARDO U., IL RITRATTO DIPINTO , IN GALASSO G., VALLET G. (A CURA DI), STORIA DEL MEZZOGIORNO, VOL. II. 2, NAPOLI 1991.

PAPPALARDO 2004   MAZZOLENI D.-PAPPALARDO U., DOMUS, PITTURA E ARCHITETTURA D'ILLUSIONE NELLA CASA ROMANA, ROMA 2004.

PAPPALARDO-GRIMALDI ET ALII 2010   PAPPALARDO U., GRIMALDI M., GIUDICE S., TROJSI G., NUOVI MOSAICI DALLA CASA DI MARCO FABIO RUFO A POMPEI, IN: ATTI DEL XV COLLO- QUIO DELL'ASSOCIAZIONE ITALIANA PER LO STUDIO E LA CONSERVAZIONE DEL MOSAICO (AQUILEIA, 4-7 FEBBRAIO 2009), TIVOLI 2010, PP. 499-509.

PAPPALARDO-CIARDIELLO 2011   PAPPALARDO U., CIARDIELLO R., MOSAICI GRECI E ROMANI, VERONA 2011

PFLUG 1989   PFLUG H., RÖMISCHE PORTRÄTSTELEN IN OBERITALIEN, MAINZ 1989.

POULSEN 1962   POULSEN V., LES PORTRAITS ROMAINS, COPENAGHEN 1962, P. 39SS.

RAGGHIANTI 1963   RAGGHIANTI C.L., PITTORI DI POMPEI, MILANO 1963.

RICHTER 1968   RICHTER G.M., "REALISMUS IN DER GRIECHISCHEN PORTRÄTKUNST", DAS ALTERTUM 14, PP. 146-157.

RODENWALDT 1909   RODENWALDT G., DIE KOMPOSITION DER POMPEJANISCHEN WAND- GEMÄLDE, BERLINO 1909.

ROMIZZI 2006   ROMIZZI L., PROGRAMMI DECORATIVI DI III E IV STILE A POMPEI, NAPOLI 2006.

ROUVERET 1981   ROUVERET A. (A CURA DI), PLINE L'ANCIEN. HISTORIE NATURELLE. LIVRE XXXVI, PARIS 1981.

SAURON 2007   SAURON G., LA PITTURA ALLEGORICA A POMPEI. LO SGUARDO DI CICERONE, MILANO 2007.

SAURON 2010   SAURON G., IL GRANDE AFFRESCO DELLA VILLA DEI MISTERI A POMPEI. MEMORIE DI UNA DEVOTA DI DIONISO, MILANO 2010.

SAURON 2013   SAURON G., UNE FRESQUE EN VOIE DE GUÉRISON: LA MÉGALOGRAPHIE DE BOSCOREALE, IN BARBET A., VERBANCK-PIÉRARD A. (A CURA DI), LA VILLA ROMAINE DE BOSCOREALE ET SES FRESQUES, ARLES 2013, PP. 119-129.

SCHEFOLD 1952   SCHEFOLD K., POMPEJANISCHE MALEREI, BASEL 1952.

SCHEFOLD 1957   SCHEFOLD K., DIE WÄNDE POMPEJIS, BERLIN 1957.

SCHEFOLD 1975   SCHEFOLD K., SPUREN ALEXANDRINISCHEN THEOLOGIE IN RÖEMISCHEN WANDMALEREIEN, IN WORT UND BILD. STUDIEN ZUR GEGENWART DER AN- TIKE, MAINZ 1975, PP. 111-123.

SCHWEITZER 1948   SCHWEITZER B., DIE BILDNISKUNST DER RÖMISCHEN REPUBLIK , LEIPZIG 1948.

SETTIS 2008   SETTIS S., ARTEMIDORO: UN PAPIRO DAL I AL XXI SECOLO, TORINO, 2008.

SETTIS 2012   GALLAZZI C., KRAMER B., S. SETTIS, INTORNO AL PAPIRO DI ARTEMIDORO, II. GEOGRAFIA E CARTOGRAFIA. ATTI DEL CONVEGNO INTERNAZIONALE DEL 27 NOVEMBRE 2009 PRESSO LA SOCIETÀ GEOGRAFICA ITALIANA, VILLA CE- LIMONTANA, ROMA, MILANO, 2012.

TRAN TAM TINH 1974   TRAN TAM TINH V., CATALOGUE DES PEINTURES ROMAINES (LATIUM ET CAMPANIE) DU MUSÉE DU LOUVRE, PARIS 1974.

TUCCINARDI 2015   TUCCINARDI M., L'ALBERO SECCO NEL MOSAICO POMPEIANO DI ALESSANDRO MAGNO, IN RIVISTA DI ENGRAMMA N. 124, 2015.

VARONE 1997   VARONE A., POMPEI: IL QUADRO HELBIG 1445, "KASPERL IM KINDERTHEATER", UNA NUOVA REPLICA E IL PROBLEMA DELLE COPIE E DELLE VARIANTI, IN I TEMI FIGURATIVI 1997, PP. 149-152.

VARONE 1998   VARONE A. UN PITTORE AL LAVORO A POMPEI, IN ROMANA PICTURA 1998, PP. 302-303.

VARONE 2002   VARONE A, L'INSULA DEI CASTI AMANTI (IX, 12), IN F. COARELLI (A CURA DI), POMPEI. LA VITA RITROVATA, UDINE 2002, PP. 334-345.

VOLLENWEIDER 1972   VOLLENWEIDER M.L., PORTRÄTGEMMEN DER RÖMISCHEN REPUBLIK, MAINZ 1972.

VON BOTHMER 1988   VON BOTHMER B., EGYPTIAN ANTECEDENTS OF ROMAN REPUBLICAN VERISM, IN: N. BONACASA - G. RIZZA (A CURA DI), RITRATTO UFFICIALE E RITRATTO PRIVATO. ATTI II CONF. INTERNAZ. RITRATTO ROMANO, ROMA 1988, PP. 47-65.

VON HEINZE 1974   VON HEINZE H., (A CURA DI), RÖMISCHE PORTRÄTS, DARMSTADT, (RISTAMPA ANTOLOGICA DI SAGGI FONDAMENTALI APPARSI FRA IL XVII ED IL XX SECOLO) 1974.

VON KASCHNITZ WEINBERG 1965   VON KASCHNITZ WEINBERG G., RÖMISCHE BILDNISSE, IN: AUSGEWÄHLTE SCHRIFTEN, BERLIN 1965.

WALLACE-HADRILL 1994   WALLACE-HADRILL A., HOUSES AND SOCIETY IN POMPEII AND HERCULANEUM, PRINCETON 1994.

WINKES 1969   WINKES R., CLIPEATA IMAGO. STUDIEN ZU EINER RÖMISCHEN BILDNISFORM, BONN 1969.

WINSOR LEACH 1990   WINSOR LEACH E., THE POLITIC OF SELF-PRESENTATION: PLINY'S LETTERS AND ROMAN PORTRAIT SCULPTURE, CLASSANTIQUITY 9, 1, 1990, PP. 14-39, TAVV. 1-14.

ZANKER 1983   ZANKER P., ZUR BILDNISREPRSENTATION FÜHRENDEN MÄNNER, IN: LES BOURGIOISIES MUNICIPALES ITALIENNES. COLLOQUIO CENTRE J.BÉRARD, NAPOLI 7- 10.XII.1981, NAPOLI 1983, PP. 251-256.

ZANKER 1989   ZANKER P., AUGUSTO E IL POTERE DELLE IMMAGINI, TORINO 1989.

ZANKER 1997   ZANKER P., LA MASCHERA DI SOCRATE, TORINO 1997.

ZEVI 1991   ZEVI F., LA PITTURA POPOLARE, IN: AA.VV., LA PITTURA DI POMPEI, MI- LANO 1991, PP. 267-273.

ZEVI 2007   ZEVI F., EPILOGO, IN J.P. MORET (A CURA DI), VILLAS, MAISONS, SANCTUAIRES ET TOMBEAUX TARDO-RÉPUBLICAINS: DECOUVERTES ET RELECTURES RECENTES: ATTI DEL CONVEGNO INTERNAZIONALE SULLA PITTURA DI II STILE IN ETÀ TARDO REPUBBLICANA, ROMA 2007, PP. 519-527.

FONTI:

VITRUVIO, DE ARCHITECTURA, EDIZIONE CURATA DA LUCIANO MIGOTTO, PADOVA 1990.

PLINIO IL VECCHIO, NATURALIS HISTORIA (LIBRI XXXV – XXXVI), EDIZIONE CURATA DA SILVIO FERRI, MILANO 2001.

LUCIANO DI SAMOSATA, ΕἸΚΌΝΕΣ, EDIZIONE CURATA DA SONIA MAFFEI, TORINO 1994.

"伟大属于罗马"

丁宁　北京大学教授

爱伦·坡曾一往情深地写过这样的诗句："光荣属于希腊，伟大属于罗马。"（To the glory that was Greece/And the grandeur that was Rome.）古希腊文明确实深深地惠及古罗马文明，以至于在很大程度上后者的崇尚与模仿（或复制）为前者的存世流布做出了无可替代的历史性贡献。不过，与此同时，古罗马艺术也不啻是对古希腊文明的继承而已，还有其空前绝后的创造。

据考证，古代罗马最初只是意大利半岛台伯河沿岸的一些村庄部落，并在约公元前754年建立了罗马城，成为了独立的国家。公元前509年，罗马废除王政，进入共和时期，一直延续到公元前31年。这500年中，罗马从一个小小的城邦，逐步发展成为威震地中海地区、横跨欧亚非三大洲的霸主，其疆域之大从地中海成为"罗马人的内湖"的说法中就可见一斑。

古希腊与古罗马

古希腊的文明很早就传播到了意大利，尤其是南部的那不勒斯以及西西里岛。同时，征战四方、不断凯旋的罗马军队频频带回大量的希腊艺术品、书籍和俘虏。于是，希腊文化就在罗马显现出更为直接和不可抵御的魅力。希腊的艺术品是罗马的贵族家庭中的珍贵收藏和装饰品，而被俘虏的希腊知识分子有的则成了罗马贵族家中的仆人兼家庭教师。罗马的上层社会开始希腊化。因而，罗马的艺术也接受着古希腊的诸种影响。

《维纳斯的背影》（详见图录编号60）是约公元前3世纪到公元前2世纪的雕像，佚失了的古希腊原作可能为青铜材质。这是继普拉克西特列斯（Praxiteles）《尼多斯的阿佛洛狄忒》（约公元前350年）之后出现的又一尊爱与美的女神的新形象，虽然作者不详，来源地不详（大希腊

区域或小亚细亚），却充分凸显了希腊化时期的审美趣味。我们看到，刚刚沐浴完的阿佛洛狄忒转过身体，回头向身后顾盼，仿佛是在欣赏她自己的身体在水中的倒影——这无疑是一种人物姿态更为自在也更为复杂的造型，引来过无数的模仿，频频出现在古代宝石饰品和青铜小雕像上。然而，将这尊雕像命名为《美臀阿佛洛狄忒》（Venus Kallipygia）其实是有点张冠李戴了，因为那是曾经在公元前2世纪时陈列在叙拉古（Siracusa）的一座神殿里的另一件作品。《维纳斯的背影》是16世纪时在罗马被发现的。尽管18世纪的雕塑家卡洛·阿尔巴奇尼（Carlo Albacini，1734 — 1813）对雕像的头部、肩膀、左臂与衣饰、右手以及右小腿等进行了修复，于今看来均不尽如人意，但是，雕像依然葆有无穷魅力，令人遐想古希腊原作的迷人风采。

《俯身的阿佛洛狄忒与厄洛斯》也是古罗马的复制品，其模仿的原作可能出自代达沙斯（Doidalsas, c. 310 BC – after 250BC）之手。在这里，美丽丰腴的阿佛洛狄忒受惊似地将头向右侧转去，目光落在小爱神的身上——这种造型要具有令人惊艳的美感，对艺术家着实是个不小的挑战。如果没有足够的解剖学知识与驾驭雕琢工具的高超能力，是断难塑造出这样充满了复杂多变的人体曲线的作品的。正像有的学者所指出的那样，这种裸体的造型既是对普拉克西特列斯《尼多斯的阿佛洛狄忒》的沐浴主题的呼应，同时又不再是正面全裸的样子了，由此增添了一种更加妩媚与亲和的意味，换一句话说，它既不像是人们膜拜的神，也不是献祭品，而更是对人本身的极致之美的塑造。

正是由于古希腊年代更为久远，流传于世的作品不太多，而且大多呈残缺状，而得益于古罗马的模仿与复制，后人才有可能相对完整地瞥见古希腊艺术的灿烂光辉。没有罗马，也就没有温克尔曼的《古代艺术史》。

万神殿

古罗马建筑艺术

当然，最能体现古罗马精神的无疑是那些具有纪念性的建筑和雕塑。

建筑如果是纪念性的，就往往会成为力量和荣誉的表征。几乎所有的古罗马建筑物都追求宏伟的规模和牢固的结构，有时私人的住宅也是如此。

最大也最出名的建筑是罗马的万神殿。它的立面是由一个三角形的山墙和希腊式的柱廊所构成的。最令人惊叹的是其圆拱顶，直径达到了44米，与建筑物的高度相仿。为了支撑这一庞然大物，大殿的墙的底部达到6米之厚。

万神殿由两部份组成的：一是传统的长方形神殿走廊，矗立着粗大的科林斯式的花岗岩石柱，另一部分则是一个巨大的圆顶大厅。门廊的长方形与大厅的圆形构成一种鲜明的对比。人们经由各种严谨而又凝重的方形结构所组成的幽暗空间，再进入敞亮的圆厅世界，就仿佛觉得自己到了天体般浑然的无限之中，心灵受到极大的震撼。灿烂的阳光从拱顶上的大圆孔（直径约为9米的圆孔）中投射下来，随时都有光影的变化，也为圆厅增添了流光溢彩的生气。建筑物内部壁面及石柱均为大理石，有些带有蓝色、紫色和橘黄色的纹路。这的确是一个充满和谐之美的宏大建筑。

古罗马雕刻艺术

人物雕塑是古罗马艺术中的极品。它不同于希腊雕像的唯美、优雅和理想化的趋势，而是酷似真人，且个性鲜明。研究表明，古罗马人从很早时起就发展了一种公共艺术。他们几乎在每一次重大战事胜利之后就要建造弘扬权势和力量的凯旋门，置于军队必经之道上，上面大多刻有歌功颂德的浮雕。而且，门的顶部往往会安置一尊皇帝驾驭战车的青铜雕像（如今多荡然无存）。正是在这些具有明显叙述性的雕塑中，罗马人显现出了特有的优势。而且，罗马人也把政治与军事领袖的大型雕像放置在公共场所中，这和希腊人将竞技英雄的雕像陈列在神殿中是相似的做法。

《奥古斯都像》是罗马帝国前期非常有代表性的帝王全身像。

公元前27年，屋大维被元老院授予"奥古斯都"（"至圣至尊"的意思）的称号，成为罗马的独裁者。这尊出土于罗马近郊的雕像塑造的就是这一罗马帝国缔造者的形象。奥古斯都面部的表情严峻而沉着，透露出帝王的尊严和高贵。他的身材魁梧，披挂着华丽的罗马式盔甲，盔甲上的浮雕描绘的是大地母神，象征着对天下的统治。奥古斯都的右手指向前方，似乎正在向部下示意，左手则握着象征权力的节杖。在他的右脚边，有一个骑在海豚上的小爱神丘比特的形象，表明奥古斯都不仅是一个伟大的统帅，同时也是一位仁爱之君。

这座雕像确实有不少值得重视的特点。第一，它注入了罗马人的自然主义倾向，不再像希腊雕塑那样选取理想化的脸形，而是将现实中的英雄奥古斯都的头像塑造出来；第二，英雄不再是裸体的形象，反而穿上了盔甲，全副武装起来，这当然是出于增强身为皇帝的奥古斯都的尊严感的考虑；第三，艺术家显然意识到了雕塑对象的身份——军事统治者——的特殊性，通过右手的姿势和炯炯有神的眼睛提供了一种前进的方向感。这和古希腊雕像也是有区别的。当然，美化的迹象也仍然显而易见。现实中的奥古斯都皇帝是体弱多病的，而且矮小跛脚，不可能像雕像那样显得高大健美。同时，他的脸部也太像希腊雕像中的阿波罗，因而也可认为是一种美化的结果。

罗马艺术中浮雕也占有重要的地位，罗马的统治者们为了炫耀他们在战争中的丰功伟绩，就往往要修建一些独立的纪功柱。其中现存最著名的当推《图拉真纪功柱》。

《卡拉卡拉像》，约 211—217 年，大理石，高 50 厘米，那不勒斯国家考古博物馆

异国风光等，都是历史研究的视觉文献，尤为难得。这是西方浮雕中的一件无以超越的巨作。

最后，我们要看一看纯粹的肖像画般的雕塑作品。

卡拉卡拉是罗马的皇帝，因为喜欢高卢族的外套（即"卡拉卡拉"）而得此名。历史上，他的残忍无以复加，人人皆知。211年即位后，他就频频地发动侵略战争，并吞了亚美尼亚。为了巩固其独揽大权的地位，他谋杀了自己的弟弟，并将其追随者二万多人统统处死。217年，他在准备另一次战争时被自己手下的护卫军将领暗杀，在位不过七年。

艺术家是在卡拉卡拉在位时雕塑这一作品的，可以想见雕刻的难度所在。但是，艺术家似乎丝毫没有丢弃肖像雕塑的真实性原则，相反，他直截了当地刻画出了卡拉卡拉内在的残忍性格。

雕像中，卡拉卡拉微侧着头，深藏在前额眉头下的双眼流露出疑虑、猜忌和不安，仿佛是在捕捉或是思忖着什么。卷曲的头发和络腮胡须围绕着凶横的脸，犹如其内心的波澜。这是对一个暴君的绝妙写照。

古罗马绘画艺术

古罗马绘画留存至今的只有壁画，而这又与维苏威火山的爆发有关。公元79年，火山喷发并淹没了庞贝和赫库兰尼姆。建筑物中的壁画由此得以幸存。直到18世纪考古学家才把它们挖掘出来。由于熔浆的覆盖，当时屋内的许多壁画被完好保存了下来。

神秘别墅中的壁画描绘的是一个与祭拜酒神的仪式活动有关的场所。在暗红色的背景上，差不多真人大小的人物形象轮廓鲜明，色彩丰富，显得颇为突出。他们仿佛是在舞台上，其姿态可能借鉴了古希腊艺术，而圆润的躯体，优雅的体态和专注的表情都透发出强烈的戏剧性效果。

人物形象的造型有着明显的希腊意味。不过，画面传达的情绪却是极为特殊和意味深长的。例如，翩然起舞的少女显露出肃穆、迷茫而又有些紧张的神情，仿佛在经历一种震撼灵魂的重大事件。

《采花的少女》是一幅优美无比的壁画。在这一依然可以看出希腊化影响的壁画里，人们感觉到的是一种极为抒

它是公元113年为了庆贺图拉真皇帝公元2世纪两次大败达契亚（今罗马尼亚）之战而竖立的，极其高大宏伟，仅底座就有两层楼高。石柱外围装饰有螺旋形大理石浮雕带，从柱子的底部盘旋而上，总长达180多米，具有生动的、如画般的叙述性。为了矫正自下而上的视差，浮雕带的宽度越向上越宽（底部一圈为89厘米，而顶端一圈为125厘米），共23圈。顶上是图拉真的圆雕像（后来在16世纪被替换为使徒彼得像）。

浮雕上出现的人物有2500多个，图拉真皇帝的出场往往被安排在困境当头时，共达90多次。就内容划分，叙述了150多个故事，从出征前的宗教仪式、皇帝的训示，两支军队的作战，直到图雷真率部下凯旋，几乎所有战争中的重要情节均一一展示，复杂的场景、众多的人物，以及叙述的连接等都安排得浑然一体，气势非凡。毫无疑义，《图拉真纪功柱》和其他古罗马的雕塑作品一样，具有重要的纪实的特征。浮雕中的人物的容貌、作战器械、服饰以及

《采花的少女》，约公元前 60 年，高约 30 厘米，那不勒斯国家考古博物馆

情的自然主义。画中的少女款款走过，采花的动作优雅、妩媚。尽管人们无法看到她的美丽容貌，但是，背对的形象却会引发观者更为微妙的遐思。鲜花与少女几乎是无法分开的美的存在。确实，这样的描绘是一种对人物形象的内心世界的一种巧妙处理。

《持笔的少女》是一幅极为难得的作品。它可能是具有写实意义的肖像画。艺术家的技巧在明暗处理上显得尤为高超，使得人物脖子和衣褶具有生动的立体感；圆形的头饰和卷发与画面的圆形相呼应。至于人物的表情，此时显然是一种认真沉思的神态。

《有桃子的静物画》是一幅小的壁画作品。具有错觉效果的写实描绘达到了一种惊人惊叹的高度。光影的投射（包括透过物体后的效果）、明暗的对比都似乎是无可挑剔的。玻璃水缸上的高光、水面的反光尤为精彩。此画是西方早期静物画的杰作。

最后，不妨提到德国文豪歌德对古罗马文明的由衷赞美："我相信罗马是全世界的学校，而我也在这里得到清洗和考验。"[3]

《持笔的少女》，1 世纪，湿壁画，直径 28.9 厘米，那不勒斯国家考古博物馆

《有桃子的静物画》，约公元 50 年，35 厘米 × 34 厘米，那不勒斯国家考古博物馆

注　释

1　See Rosanna Cappelli and Annalisa Lo Monaco, *The National Archaeological Museum of Naples: Guide,* Napoli: Electa, 2009, p. 30.

2　See R.R.R. Smith, *Hellenistic Sculpture*, London: Thames & Hudson, 1991, p. 80.

3　Goethe, *Italian Journey*, 1786-1788, translated by Auden & Mayer, San Fracisco: North Point Press, 1982, pp. 137-138.

"The Grandeur That Was Rome"

Ding Ning   Professor of Peking University

The ancient Greek civilization indeed exerted profound and positive influence on ancient Rome, to such an extent that the latter's veneration and imitation of art made an irreplaceable contribution to the preservation and continuity of the ancient Greek civilization. On the other hand, Roman art was not merely an inheritance of Greek civilization, but also an unprecedented creation.

Given the antiquity of the ancient Greek civilization, not many of its works have survived to the present day, and those that have are often in a state of disrepair. The Roman's imitation and replication enabled future generations to glimpse the luminous splendor of ancient Greek art in a relatively complete form.

Among the surviving Roman works, the commemorative buildings and sculptures epitomize the spirit of Rome at its zenith. These works are often seen as expressions of power and honor. Roman architecture, known for its grandiosity and robustness, was a testament to this ethos, with even private residences reflecting this trend.

The figurative sculptures of ancient Rome represent some of the finest achievements of Roman art. In contrast to the aesthetic, elegant, and idealized tendencies of Greek statues, Roman sculptures were remarkable for their lifelike realism and distinctive individualistic character.

The only surviving examples of Roman painting are the frescos, the preservation of which can be attributed to the eruption of Mount Vesuvius in 79 CE. This catastrophic event engulfed the cities of Pompeii and Herculaneum, preserving the murals within the buildings. These works, excavated by archaeologists in the 18th century, offer an invaluable insight into the art of that period.

Lastly, the profound admiration for ancient Roman civilization expressed by the German literary luminary, Johann Wolfgang von Goethe, merits mention: "I believe that Rome is the school for the whole world and I, too, have been purged and tested here." His words capture the enduring influence and appeal of the ancient Roman civilization.

Socrates: *Then are not all beautiful things beautiful by the beautiful?*
Hippias: *Yes, by the beautiful.*
S: *By the beautiful, which is something?*
H: *Yes, for what alternative is there?*
S: *"Tell me, then, stranger," he will say, "what is this, the beautiful?"*
......
S: *So I think, Hippias, that I have been benefited by conversation with both of you; for I think I know the meaning of the proverb,*
"Beautiful things are difficult."

—— *Plato, Hippias Major*

苏格拉底：美的东西之所以美，是否也由于美？

希庇阿斯：是的，由于美。

苏格拉底：美也是一个真实的东西？

希庇阿斯：很真实，这有什么难题？

苏格拉底：我们的论敌现在就要问了："客人，请告诉我什么是美？"

......

苏格拉底：......至少是从我和你们俩的讨论中，希庇阿斯，我得到了一个益处，那就是更清楚地了解一句谚语：

"美是难的。"

—— [古希腊] 柏拉图《大希庇阿斯篇》

序　言

　　美是什么？美是客观的，还是主观的？在《大希庇阿斯篇》中，柏拉图分析并批判了古希腊各种有关美的观点，而其中苏格拉底的一句感叹——"美是难的"，成为后人追寻美学之源的起点。

　　那不勒斯国家考古博物馆珍藏了众多精美的古罗马藏品，尤以玻璃器、青铜器、彩绘壁画、雕刻、雕塑为优。两千年前，那不勒斯东海岸的维苏威火山剧烈喷发，泥流与火山灰将庞贝、赫库兰尼姆与斯塔比亚等一众古罗马城市深埋其下。直到18世纪中叶，考古学家的发掘使它们重见天日，特殊的埋藏环境完美地保存了这些精美文物。火山灰下的珍贵遗迹、遗物忠实记录了这个伟大文明的审美情趣，并使我们有机会去理解古罗马人对于美的思考。

Foreword

What is beauty? Is it objective or subjective? In *Hippias Major*, Plato analyzed and criticized various theories on beauty. Socrates' conclusive exclamation, "beautiful things are difficult", became the starting point of the pursuit of aesthetic theory for the later generation.

The National Archaeological Museum of Naples houses many exquisite ancient Roman artifacts, including glassware, bronze ware, painted murals, carvings, and sculptures. Two thousand years ago, the eruption of Mount Vesuvius engulfed a group of ancient Roman cities such as Pompeii, Herculaneum, and Stabiae under volcanic ash. These magnificent pieces, once buried under the ash, were excavated by archaeologists in the the eighteenth century century, and have been preserved in their pristine state ever since. Beyond their visual appeal, these artifacts also offer a window into the ancient Roman world, revealing the culture, aesthetic values, and beliefs of a civilization that flourished over two thousand years ago.

1

斜倚的阿佛洛狄忒
Statue of Leaning Aphrodite

大理石
高 148 厘米，宽 58 厘米，厚 44 厘米
公元 2 世纪
罗马
那不勒斯国家考古博物馆藏，编号 6396

Marble
h 148 cm, w 58 cm, d 44 cm
2nd century CE
Rome
National Archaeological Museum of Naples,
inv. 6396

　　这座雕塑原本位于一个具有一定高度的壁龛内，古罗马人巧妙地利用建筑构件将阿佛洛狄忒置于"画框"之中，使得观者只能从下往上仰视女神。这种雕塑与人物的互动关系，在一定程度上体现了古罗马的人神观念。

　　在雕塑的表现上，阿佛洛狄忒头戴连帽斗篷，遮蔽头部，塑造出部分阴影面，为雕塑增添了一丝神秘的韵味。这种带有"雨天"氛围的设计可以追溯到公元前5世纪，古罗马人在安敦尼时期对这种风格的复刻，在彰显女神摄人心魄的美丽容颜与体态之余，更表现出古罗马人对古典美的推崇。阿佛洛狄忒左手肘轻轻依靠立柱，体态微倾，但上举微微捻住连帽斗篷的右手让雕塑的重心保持了微妙的平衡。向前半步的左腿仿佛在迎向瞻仰她的观者，女神的灵韵迎面而来。

　　最新的考古学研究表明，这座雕塑有明显的着色痕迹，表明它曾拥有鲜明的色彩，这其实有利于观者更好地理解作品与周围建筑的关系。不难想象，千年前，一个明媚的午后，阳光倾泻在阿佛洛狄忒的身上，在壁龛和雕塑本身阴影的衬托下，女神的美划破了光与影的界限，也划破了虚与实的边界。

I

美 的 承 继

THE INHERITANCE OF BEAUTY

传说，特洛伊城陷落后，埃涅阿斯漂泊数年，终于行抵意大利半岛。经过无数次征战，这个曾经的失意地逐渐成为了西方世界的中心——罗马帝国。两千六百年后，埃德加·爱伦·坡在《致海伦》中写道："光荣属于希腊，伟大属于罗马。"这句话深刻表现了西方世界对于古罗马的推崇。这个尚武的民族在征服和扩张的过程中，为帝国带来了广袤的疆域、稳定的生活环境与无尽的财富，更承接并延续了古希腊的哲学思想。

殷实的物质基础与丰饶的精神基础是古罗马美学的根基。借由古罗马人民的双手，数座绝美之城傲然而立，成为整个地中海的瑰宝。

According legend, after the fall of Troy, Aeneas wandered for several years before finally arriving on the Italian peninsula. Through countless battles, this land gradually became the center of the Western world–the heart of Roman Empire. Edgar Allan Poe profoundly expressed the West's admiration for ancient Rome in his work "To Helen" writing, "To the glory that was Greece, and the grandeur that was Rome." Through conquest and expansion, this nation with strong military and power ethos gained vast territories, a stable living environment, and endless wealth to its people, while also inheriting and continuing the philosophical ideas of ancient Greece.

The solid material foundation and abundant spiritual basis became the cornerstone of ancient Roman aesthetics. The beautiful cities built by the Romans, who aspired to beauty, became the treasures of the entire Mediterranean region.

Remember, Roman, these will be your arts:
to teach the ways of peace to those you conquer,
to spare defeated peoples, tame the proud.

—— *Vergil, The Aeneid*

"罗马的艺术应该是将和平强加于人的艺术，是施行法治的艺术，是给战败者以宽恕、使傲慢者屈服的艺术。"

——[古罗马] 维吉尔《埃涅阿斯纪》

2

战士头盔
Warrior's Helmet

青铜
高 28 厘米，宽 21 厘米
公元前 5 至公元前 4 世纪
意大利南部
那不勒斯国家考古博物馆藏，编号 5749

Bronze
h 28 cm, w 21 cm
5th-4th century BCE
Southern Italy
National Archaeological Museum of Naples, *inv. 5749*

　　此藏品一般被认为是早期头部护具的雏形。它来自意大利南部地区，当地居民（包括萨莫奈人、卢卡尼亚人、梅萨比人）在与古希腊文明的接触中获得了武器制造方面的技艺和模式，同时也在不断进行文化的吸纳与交融。

3

战利品前的胜利女神与国王
Fresco with Nike and King in front of a Trophy

彩绘壁画
高 54 厘米，宽 53.5 厘米，厚 7 厘米
公元 1 世纪
庞贝
那不勒斯国家考古博物馆藏，编号 8843

Painted fresco
h 54 cm, w 53.5 cm, d 7 cm
1ˢᵗ century CE
Pompeii
National Archaeological Museum of Naples,
inv. 8843

　　这幅壁画中央的角形头盔和圆形盾牌皆是高卢人所使用的武器，但它们已经成为马其顿人的战利品，画面左侧的胜利女神尼克和右侧凯旋的将领共同诠释了这一情景。

　　胜利女神右手手持战利品之一的斧头，衣着的颜色至今仍然鲜丽。而在画面另一侧与女神对望的年轻男性，正是凯旋的亚历山大大帝。画中的亚历山大，是一个刚刚加冕的年轻君主，他身披象征马其顿国王身份的盔甲，盔甲上的蛇发女妖和胜利女神脚边的头盔都能证实其身份。同时，他左手手持马其顿长枪，右手拿着象征军队指挥官的权杖，昭示着胜利的无尽荣耀。

4

赫丘利小雕像
Small Statue of Hercules

青铜   Bronze
高 9 厘米，宽 4 厘米，厚 3 厘米   h 9 cm, w 4 cm, d 3 cm
公元 1 世纪   1st century CE
赫库兰尼姆   Herculaneum
那不勒斯国家考古博物馆藏，   National Archaeological Museum of Naples,
编号 5042   inv. 5042

5

赫丘利小雕像
Small Statue of Hercules

青铜   Bronze
高 17 厘米，宽 9 厘米   h 17 cm, w 9 cm
公元 1 世纪   1st century CE
维苏威火山遗址   Vesuvian area
那不勒斯国家考古博物馆藏   National Archaeological Museum of Naples

6

赫拉克勒斯头像
Herma of Heracles

青铜
高 63 厘米，宽 35 厘米，厚 27 厘米
公元 1 世纪
赫库兰尼姆
那不勒斯国家考古博物馆藏，编号 5594

Bronze
h 63 cm, w 35 cm, d 27 cm
1st century CE
Herculaneum
National Archaeological Museum of Naples,
inv. 5594

7

穿板甲的路奇乌斯·维鲁斯雕像
Statue of Lucio Vero with Armour Plate

大理石
高 220 厘米，宽 100 厘米，厚 69 厘米
公元 1 至 2 世纪
罗马
那不勒斯国家考古博物馆藏，编号 6081

Marble
h 220 cm, w 100 cm, d 69 cm
1st-2nd century CE
Rome
National Archaeological Museum of Naples, *inv. 6081*

在西方近代早期的古董交易中，总是倾向于去
修复那些缺少头部或其他身体部位的雕塑。修复中，
人们经常将不同地区、不同风格的作品重塑为一个整
体。这件完成于公元1世纪朱里亚·克劳狄时期雕像
本身仅留存下身着盔甲的躯干。当它在弗拉斯卡蒂
（Frascati）被发现后，著名的雕塑修复师卡洛·阿尔
巴西尼（1734—1813）借鉴公元2世纪罗马帝国皇帝
路奇乌斯·维鲁斯的肖像对其进行了修复。

8

色雷斯角斗士头盔

Helmet of a Tracian

青铜
高 47 厘米，宽 40 厘米，厚 43 厘米
公元 1 世纪
庞贝
那不勒斯国家考古博物馆藏，编号 5650

Bronze
h 47 cm, w 40 cm, d 43 cm
1st century CE
Pompeii
National Archaeological Museum of Naples, *inv. 5650*

角斗士在竞技中需要配备各种武器和盔甲，其样式往往与他们自己的民族在战争时期所使用的武器类似。这件宽边且带有顶饰的色雷斯角斗士头盔，前额饰有令人不寒而栗的美杜莎图案，她正是蛇发女妖三姐妹中最为人熟知的一位。美杜莎这一符号的使用，代表着她对于角斗士的保护，庇佑他们抵御邪恶，远离死亡。

9

油罐
Oil Container

青铜
高 11 厘米，宽 7 厘米
公元 1 世纪
庞贝
那不勒斯国家考古博物馆藏，编号 69970

Bronze
h 11 cm, w 7 cm
1ˢᵗ century CE
Pompeii
National Archaeological Museum of Naples, *inv. 69970*

10

刮身板
Strigil

青铜
高 3 厘米，宽 10 厘米，厚 20 厘米
公元 1 世纪
庞贝
那不勒斯国家考古博物馆藏，编号 70079

Bronze
h 3 cm, w 10 cm, d 20 cm
1ˢᵗ century CE
Pompeii
National Archaeological Museum of Naples, *inv. 70079*

油罐和刮身板都是最基础的体育用品。比赛前，
摔跤手会用橄榄油涂抹身体，比赛后则会用刮身板清
洁身体，刮掉身上的橄榄油和汗水。

11

绘有战斗场景的壁画
Fresco with a Scene of a Fight

彩绘壁画
高 117 厘米，宽 82 厘米，厚 19.5 厘米
公元 1 世纪
斯卡法蒂
那不勒斯国家考古博物馆藏，编号 134059

Painted fresco
h 117 cm, w 82 cm, d 19.5 cm
1ˢᵗ century CE
Scafati
National Archaeological Museum of Naples, *inv. 134059*

1912年9月26日，那不勒斯国家考古博物馆以500里拉的低价购藏了这幅壁画以及硬币和其他物品。壁画背景中的红色已有褪色痕迹，但不难想见其原本亮丽的颜色。在红色背景的衬托下，两位年轻的摔跤手在黄色地面的棕色区域对峙，该区域仅由几笔轻巧的笔触勾勒而成，但在衬托下，两位摔跤手角力的力量感喷薄而出。仔细观察画面的底部，可以发现原来的黄色"地毯"边纹，经过漫长的岁月，如今仅存下方边缘部分。

当这幅壁画被发现时，它正置于小型浴场中高温浴池的半圆形小室内。根据壁画所描绘的运动场景推测，这座小型浴场可能由运动场所改建而来。

12

绘有手持配重的跳跃场景壁画
Fresco with Jumping Scene with Halteres

彩绘壁画
高 79 厘米，宽 218 厘米，厚 16 厘米
公元 1 世纪
庞贝
那不勒斯国家考古博物馆藏

Painted fresco
h 79 cm, w 218 cm, d 16 cm
1ˢᵗ century CE
Pompeii
National Archaeological Museum of Naples

　　这幅长达两米的壁画描绘了一幅内容丰富的运动比赛场景。画面中央绘有一个方形石柱，顶部雕刻着神祇的肖像，根据画面场景、神祇蓄须以及身旁装饰有象征胜利的棕榈叶的特征，他极有可能就是大力神赫拉克勒斯。同时，仔细观察画面的右侧，可以发现一个运动员在比赛开始前，正专注地用橄榄油擦拭自己身体，鲜明地展示了运动员备战的过程。相较于画面中央与右侧的静态场景，画面左侧则是两个动态的人物。左侧的两名运动员正手持某种类似哑铃的配重，进行跳远比赛。同时，这两位跳远的运动员在跳远时已经穿戴着摔跤手套，这在侧面证明了五项全能中跳远比赛和摔跤比赛的顺序关系。

13

墨丘利小雕像
Small Statue of Mercury

青铜
高 26 厘米，宽 11 厘米，厚 11 厘米
公元 1 世纪
维苏威火山遗址
那不勒斯国家考古博物馆藏，编号 5220

Bronze
h 26 cm, w 11 cm, d 11 cm
1st century CE
Vesuvian area
National Archaeological Museum of Naples, *inv. 5220*

14

墨丘利壁灯
Wall Lamp with Mercury

青铜
高 3 厘米，宽 9 厘米，厚 9 厘米
公元 1 世纪
维苏威火山遗址
那不勒斯国家考古博物馆藏，编号 72884

Bronze
h 3 cm, w 9 cm, d 9 cm
1st century CE
Vesuvian area
National Archaeological Museum of Naples, *inv. 72884*

15

德米特里一世头像
Head of Demetrio Poliercete

大理石
高 43 厘米，宽 30 厘米，厚 28 厘米
公元 1 世纪
赫库兰尼姆
那不勒斯国家考古博物馆藏，编号 6149

Marble
h 43 cm, w 30 cm, d 28 cm
1st century CE
Herculaneum
National Archaeological Museum of Naples, *inv. 6149*

16

安提玛科斯 · 克罗丰头像
Head of Antimaco di Colofone

大理石
高 53 厘米，宽 33 厘米，厚 28 厘米
公元 1 世纪
赫库兰尼姆
那不勒斯国家考古博物馆藏，编号 6155

Marble
h 53 cm, w 33 cm, d 28 cm
1st century CE
Herculaneum
National Archaeological Museum of Naples, *inv. 6155*

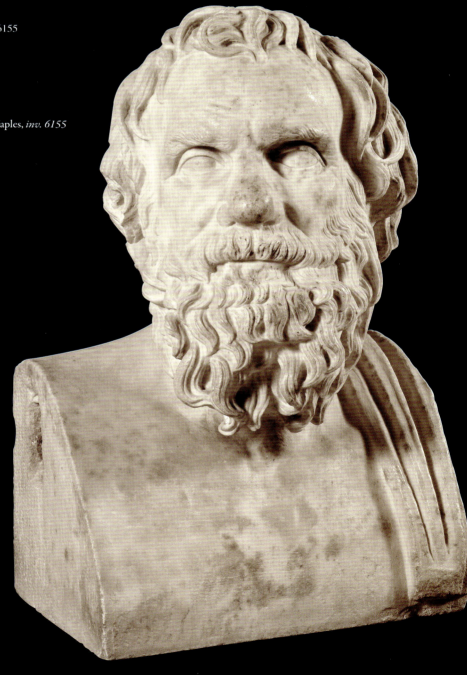

17

伪塞内卡头像
Pseudo Seneca

青铜
高 47 厘米，宽 24 厘米，厚 24 厘米
公元 1 世纪
赫库兰尼姆
那不勒斯国家考古博物馆藏，编号 5616

Bronze
h 47 cm, w 24 cm, d 24 cm
1st century CE
Herculaneum
National Archaeological Museum of Naples, *inv. 5616*

古罗马时期，在肖像塑造的对象选择上，无论是以杰出的诗人、艺术家、将领为代表的尘世凡人，还是传说中的神祇，都是被雕刻的对象。而雕塑家将他们对美的理解注入自己的作品中。其中，被称为"伪塞内卡头像"的肖像作品（出土于赫库兰尼姆）最为典型。这件作品描绘了一个面容消瘦、形容枯槁的男子，他极有可能是斯多葛学派的代表人物——塞内卡。这件作品的雕刻风格符合了长期以来塑造理想形象的创作传统，这种传统比罗马艺术中常见的现实主义表现形式更受青睐。实际上，塞内卡的真实外表是典型的富有之人的形象，他体态较同龄人更为肥胖，就这样的事实而言，塞内卡的真实相貌与其作品中斯多葛派的哲学理想并不相符。

II

生活之美

THE BEAUTY OF LIFE

帝国的繁荣和稳定是美学与艺术发展的沃土。我们经常在维苏威火山城市的住宅和公共建筑的装饰中发现日常生活的图像，它们为我们重塑了一个丰富多彩的古罗马世界。比古希腊人更甚，古罗马公民在生活的各个方面中都尽力追求精致与享受：他们用精美的器具点缀自己的家，建造宏伟的公共建筑供市民消遣娱乐，用华丽的马赛克装饰地表与墙面。

不止于物质，古罗马人更追求精神的完满，而戏剧满足了人们这样的需求。古罗马人无比重视戏剧，城市的公民齐聚于剧场之中，通过故事中的悲喜与善恶连接共同的现实与理想。

The prosperity and stability of the empire provided a fertile ground for the development of aesthetics and art. In the decorations of the houses and public buildings of the Vesuvian cities, we often find images of daily life illustrating a vivid and colorful world of ancient Roman society. More so than the ancient Greeks, ancient Roman citizens pursued refinement and enjoyment in every aspect of their lives: they adorned their houses with exquisite utensils, constructed magnificent public buildings for communal entertainment, and decorated floors and walls with elaborate mosaics.

Not only did they pursue material beauty, but the ancient Romans also sought spiritual fulfillment, finding satisfaction in theater. The Romans attached great importance to drama: citizens gathered together in theaters, connecting their shared reality and aspirations through the joys and sorrows of the stories.

Even if you speak of the beautiful you are speaking of pleasure; for beauty would hardly be beauty if it were not pleasurable.

—Epicurus

"即使你谈论的是美，你也是在谈论愉悦；因为美如果不是令人愉悦的就不会是美的。"

——［古希腊］伊壁鸠鲁

18

风景
Landscape

彩绘壁画
高 24 厘米，宽 39 厘米，厚 5 厘米
公元 1 世纪
赫库兰尼姆
那不勒斯国家考古博物馆藏，编号 9442

Painted fresco
h 24 cm, w 39 cm, d 5 cm
1st century CE
Herculaneum
National Archaeological Museum of Naples, *inv. 9442*

19

方形盥洗盆拉布罗
Labrum with Square Basin

大理石
高 78 厘米，宽 45 厘米
公元 1 世纪
维苏威火山遗址
那不勒斯国家考古博物馆藏，编号 6876

Marble
h 78 cm, w 45 cm
1ˢᵗ century CE
Vesuvian area
National Archaeological Museum of Naples, *inv. 6876*

古罗马上流社会居住的房屋被称为城市府邸（Domus）。大理石和灰泥制的各类大型装饰品奠定了房屋的审美基调。

对于古罗马人而言，房屋不仅承担了日常起居的功能，同时还是大摆筵席、招待宾朋的场所。种类繁多的生活器具点缀其中，题材多样的彩绘壁画让空间变得更加宽敞和绚丽。

20

粉饰灰泥吊顶
Ceiling Stucco

灰泥
高 78.5 厘米，宽 78.5 厘米，厚 15 厘米
公元 1 世纪
维苏威火山遗址
那不勒斯国家考古博物馆藏，编号 9634

Stucco frieze
h 78.5 cm, w 78.5 cm, d 15 cm
1st century CE
Vesuvian area
National Archaeological Museum of Naples, *inv. 9634*

21

圆形浮雕
Oscillum

大理石
高 30 厘米，厚 4 厘米
公元 1 世纪
来源未知
那不勒斯国家考古博物馆藏，编号 6553

Marble
h 30 cm, d 4 cm
1st century CE
Unknown
National Archaeological Museum of Naples, *inv. 6553*

　　在典型的罗马住宅中，除了以宁芙雕塑和喷泉作为常见的建筑装饰外，住宅的花园可能会采用壁饰装饰。这样的做法，模仿了额外的花园空间，增强住宅中的空间感，并通过打开墙壁的假象，展现出由雕像和各种本土及异国动物构成的奇幻空间，营造出一种梦幻的氛围。

　　部分建筑装饰以大理石为主要材料，其中包括这种双面圆形浮雕，它们的石料通常取材于住宅所在的城市或行省。双面圆形浮雕通常被悬挂起来，用于装饰周边廊柱的空间。这件作品一面描绘了带有蛇发女妖图案的驱邪垂饰，另一面则以音乐艺术为主题，其类似面具的造型说明了它受到了戏剧艺术的启发。

22

斯芬克斯像立于壁毯边缘（庞贝壁画第三风格）

Decoration of III Pompeian Style with Sphinx on the Edge of a Carpet

彩绘壁画
高 30 厘米，宽 36 厘米，厚 3 厘米
公元 1 世纪
庞贝
那不勒斯国家考古博物馆藏，编号 9933

Painted fresco
h 30 cm, w 36 cm, d 3 cm
1st century CE
Pompeii
National Archaeological Museum of Naples, *inv. 9933*

24

建筑隔断装饰
Fresco with Architectural Partition

彩绘壁画
高 123 厘米，宽 38 厘米，厚 7 厘米
公元 1 世纪
庞贝
那不勒斯国家考古博物馆藏，编号 9856

Painted fresco
h 123 cm, w 38 cm, d 7 cm
1st century CE
Pompeii
National Archaeological Museum of Naples, *inv. 9856*

23

建筑隔断装饰
Fresco with Architectural Partition

彩绘壁画
高 188 厘米，宽 31.5 厘米，厚 9.5 厘米
公元 1 世纪
庞贝
那不勒斯国家考古博物馆藏，编号 9772

Painted fresco
h 188 cm, w 31.5 cm, d 9.5 cm
1st century CE
Pompeii
National Archaeological Museum of Naples, *inv. 9772*

25

闺中女子
Fresco with Women in Gynoecium

彩绘壁画
高 67 厘米，宽 67 厘米，厚 7 厘米
公元 1 世纪
赫库兰尼姆
那不勒斯国家考古博物馆藏，编号 9387

Painted fresco
h 67 cm, w 67 cm, d 7m
1st century CE
Herculaneum
National Archaeological Museum of Naples, *inv. 9387*

26

灯台细节
Detail of a Candlestick

彩绘壁画
高 23 厘米，宽 15.5 厘米，厚 4 厘米
公元 1 世纪
庞贝
那不勒斯国家考古博物馆藏，编号 9600

Painted fresco
h 23 cm, w 15.5 cm, d 4 cm
1st century CE
Pompeii
National Archaeological Museum of Naples,
inv. 9600

27

灯台壁画
Fresco with Candlestick

彩绘壁画
高 164 厘米，宽 33 厘米，厚 7 厘米
公元 1 世纪
赫库兰尼姆
那不勒斯国家考古博物馆藏，编号 9765

Painted fresco
h 164 cm, w 33 cm, d 7 cm
1st century CE
Herculaneum
National Archaeological Museum of Naples,
inv. 9765

28

花园壁画
Fresco with Garden Scene

彩绘壁画
高 102 厘米，宽 39.5 厘米，厚 6 厘米
公元 1 世纪
庞贝
那不勒斯国家考古博物馆藏，编号 9761

Painted fresco
h 102 cm, w 39.5 cm, d 6 cm
1st century CE
Pompeii
National Archaeological Museum of Naples,
inv. 9761

29

灯台
Candlestick

青铜
高 130 厘米，宽 21 厘米，厚 24 厘米
公元 1 世纪
庞贝
那不勒斯国家考古博物馆藏，编号 78519

Bronze
h 130 cm, w 21cm, d 24 cm
1st century CE
Pompeii
National Archaeological Museum of Naples,
inv. 78519

30

灯台
Candlestick

青铜
高 113 厘米，宽 19 厘米，厚 21 厘米
公元 1 世纪
庞贝
那不勒斯国家考古博物馆藏，编号 78537

Bronze
h 113 cm, w 19 cm, d 21 cm
1st century CE
Pompeii
National Archaeological Museum of Naples, *inv. 78537*

　　在某些情况下，特别是在夜晚，自然光的缺乏要通过灯具来弥补。这些灯具的制作采用了陶、铅、玻璃、青铜等多种材料。同时，置于灯台顶部的油灯，内设一个腔室盛放燃料，将灯芯插入后浸泡，便可缓慢燃烧，提供持续照明。

31

双口油灯
Bilicne Oil Lamp

青铜
高 7 厘米，宽 9 厘米，厚 20 厘米
公元 1 世纪
庞贝
那不勒斯国家考古博物馆藏，编号 SN01

Bronze
h 7 cm, w 9 cm, d 20 cm
1st century CE
Pompei
National Archaeological Museum of Naples,
inv. SN01

32

有狮子头像的双口油灯
Bilicne Oil Lamp with Leonine Protome

青铜
高 7 厘米，宽 12 厘米，厚 22 厘米
公元 1 世纪
庞贝
那不勒斯国家考古博物馆藏，编号 120262

Bronze
h 7cm, w 12 cm, d 22 cm
1st century CE
Pompei
National Archaeological Museum of Naples,
inv. 120262

33

折叠三脚架
Folding Tripod

青铜
高 75 厘米，宽 45 厘米，厚 45 厘米
公元 1 世纪
庞贝
那不勒斯国家考古博物馆藏，编号 73945

Bronze
h 75cm, w 45 cm, d 45 cm
1ˢᵗ century CE
Pompeii
National Archaeological Museum of Naples,
inv. 73945

34

壳形烘焙模具
Pastry Shell Form

青铜
高 8 厘米，宽 20 厘米
公元 1 世纪
庞贝
那不勒斯国家考古博物馆藏，编号 76278

Bronze
h 8 cm, w 20 cm
1st century CE
Pompeii
National Archaeological Museum of Naples,
inv. 76278

35

便携式火盆
Portable Brazier

陶
高 18 厘米，宽 37 厘米，厚 25 厘米
公元 1 世纪
维苏威火山遗址
那不勒斯国家考古博物馆藏，编号 76/198

Terracotta
h 18 cm, w 37 cm, d 25 cm
1st century CE
Vesuvian area
National Archaeological Museum of Naples,
inv. 76/198

36

茶炉
Samovar

青铜
高 45 厘米，宽 36 厘米
公元 1 世纪
庞贝
那不勒斯国家考古博物馆藏，编号 129441

Bronze
h 45 cm, w 36 cm
1ˢᵗ century CE
Pompeii
National Archaeological Museum of Naples, *inv. 129441*

这件茶炉是古罗马人在桌子上或其他地方加热液体的器具，在罗马时代成为象征上层社会晚宴优雅与精致的标志。茶炉"腹部"的中部设有一个水龙头，顶部配有一个压力阀。这种三足茶炉既可以放在桌子上使用，也可以用链条悬挂起来，具体使用方式可根据场合灵活调整。

37

西图拉桶形瓶
Bronze vase

青铜
高 24 厘米，宽 26 厘米
公元 1 世纪
庞贝
那不勒斯国家考古博物馆藏，编号 184985

Bronze
h 24 cm, w 26 cm
1st century CE
Pompeii
National Archaeological Museum of Naples,
inv. 184985

38

水罐
Pitcher

玻璃
高 24 厘米，宽 21 厘米
公元 1 世纪
维苏威火山遗址
那不勒斯国家考古博物馆藏，编号 5371

Glass
h 24 cm, w 21 cm
1st century CE
Vesuvian area
National Archaeological Museum of
Naples, *inv. 5371*

39

瓶
Bottle

玻璃
高 22 厘米，宽 12 厘米
公元 1 世纪
庞贝
那不勒斯国家考古博物馆藏，编号 13122

Glass
h 22 cm, w 12 cm
1ˢᵗ century CE
Pompeii
National Archaeological Museum of Naples,
inv. 13122

40

浮雕玻璃杯
Glass with Ribs

玻璃
高 9 厘米，宽 9 厘米
公元 1 世纪
维苏威火山遗址
那不勒斯国家考古博物馆藏，编号 12490

Glass
h 9 cm, w 9 cm
1ˢᵗ century CE
Vesuvian area
National Archaeological Museum of Naples, *inv. 12490*

41

双柄刻纹杯
Cup Decorated with Two Handles

玻璃
高 4 厘米，宽 16 厘米
公元 1 世纪
庞贝
那不勒斯国家考古博物馆藏，
编号 133274

Glass
h 4 cm, w 16 cm
1st century CE
Pompeii
National Archaeological Museum of Naples,
inv. 133274

42

杯子与三足碟
Cup with Saucer with Three Feet

玻璃
高 11 厘米，宽 10 厘米
公元 1 世纪
庞贝
那不勒斯国家考古博物馆藏，
编号 11669（托）、11668（杯）

Glass
h 11 cm, w 10 cm
1st century CE
Pompeii
National Archaeological Museum of Naples,
inv. 11669 & 11668

43

软膏容器
Ointment Container

玻璃
高 16 厘米，宽 10 厘米
公元 1 世纪
庞贝
那不勒斯国家考古博物馆藏，编号 10236

Glass
h 16 cm, w 10 cm
1ˢᵗcentury CE
Pompeii
National Archaeological Museum of Naples,
inv. 10236

44

软膏容器
Ointment Container

玻璃
高 15 厘米，宽 4 厘米
公元 1 世纪
庞贝
那不勒斯国家考古博物馆藏，编号 128–146

Glass
h 15 cm, w 4 cm
1ˢᵗcentury CE
Pompeii
National Archaeological Museum of Naples,
inv. 128-146

45

软膏容器
Ointment Container

玻璃
高 10 厘米，宽 2 厘米
公元 1 世纪
赫库兰尼姆
那不勒斯国家考古博物馆藏，编号 113821

Glass
h 10 cm, w 2 cm
1ˢᵗcentury CE
Herculaneum
National Archaeological Museum of Naples,
inv. 113821

46

建筑物中的献贡品女性
Offering Woman inside Architecture

彩绘壁画
高 90 厘米，宽 40 厘米，厚 8 厘米
公元 1 世纪
赫库兰尼姆
那不勒斯国家考古博物馆藏，编号 9651

Painted fresco
h 90 cm, w 40 cm, d 8 cm
1ˢᵗ century CE
Herculaneum
National Archaeological Museum of Naples,
inv. 9651

献贡品的女性与雕像
Fresco with Offering Woman
and Statue

彩绘壁画
高 77 厘米，宽 58.5 厘米，厚 8 厘米
公元 1 世纪
赫库兰尼姆
那不勒斯国家考古博物馆藏，
编号 9276

Painted fresco
h 77 cm, w 58.5 cm, d 8 cm
1stcentury CE
Herculaneum
National Archaeological Museum of Naples,
inv. 9276

48

献贡品的男女
Fresco of Offering Man
and Woman

彩绘壁画
高 75 厘米，宽 90 厘米
公元 1 世纪
斯塔比亚
那不勒斯国家考古博物馆藏，
编号 8966

Painted fresco
h 75 cm, w 90 cm
1st century CE
Stabia
National Archaeological Museum of Naples,
inv. 8966

79

49

家庭守护神小雕像
Small Statue of Family God

青铜
高 19 厘米，宽 8 厘米
公元 1 世纪
维苏威火山遗址
那不勒斯国家考古博物馆藏，编号 5408

Bronze
h 19 cm, 8 cm
1ˢᵗ century CE
Vesuvian area
National Archaeological Museum of Naples, *inv. 5408*

　　罗马家庭的一个显著特色便是在房屋的各个地方摆放供奉用小神龛（lararia），尤其常见于中庭和列柱中庭之中。这些神龛中陈列着家庭守护神们的小雕像，它们往往与这个家庭自己的守护神拉尔（Lares）相伴。这些小神龛的名字正来源于拉尔。家庭守护神拉尔通常被描绘成手持角形酒器的跳舞青年。

50

幸运守护神伊西斯小雕像
Small Statue of Isis Fortune Bearer

青铜
高 15 厘米，宽 6 厘米
公元 1 世纪
维苏威火山遗址
那不勒斯国家考古博物馆藏，编号 5344

Bronze
h 15 cm, w 6 cm
1ˢᵗ century CE
Vesuvian area
National Archaeological Museum of Naples, *inv. 5344*

阿斯克勒庇俄斯
Farnese Aclepius

大理石
高 232 厘米，宽 108 厘米，厚 50 厘米
公元 2 世纪
罗马
那不勒斯国家考古博物馆藏，编号 6360

Marble
h 232 cm, w 108 cm, d 50 cm
2nd century CE
Rome
National Archaeological Museum of Naples, *inv. 6360*

医药之神阿斯克勒庇俄斯是光明之神阿波罗与凡人公主科洛尼斯之子。他继承了父亲阿波罗高超的治愈能力，曾让亡者起死回生，却因此被众神之王宙斯用雷霆击杀，并在死后化身为蛇夫座。

在这尊雕像中，阿斯克勒庇俄斯仅身披一件名为希玛纯（himation）的大长袍，他伟岸的身躯直观地展现出身体中强大的力量。他左脚旁的圆锥形神石名叫翁法洛斯（omphalos），这件器物与阿波罗的信仰体系相关，暗示着阿斯克勒庇俄斯与其父阿波罗的关联。他的右手握着一根被蛇缠绕的手杖，这是医药之神的象征。手杖上蜕皮的蛇象征着阿斯克勒庇俄斯所拥有的双重力量：医学知识（治愈之杖）与赋予新生的能力。

有酒神雕像和贡盘的静物画
Still Life with Offers for Dionysus

彩绘壁画
高 69 厘米，宽 71 厘米，厚 8 厘米
公元 1 世纪
赫库兰尼姆
那不勒斯国家考古博物馆藏，编号 8615

Painted fresco
h 69 cm, w 71 cm, d 8 cm
1ˢᵗ century CE
Herculaneum
National Archaeological Museum of Naples,
inv. 8615

这幅静物壁画描绘了献给酒神狄俄尼索斯的贡品。画面左侧庄重伫立的镀金青铜小雕像就是酒神的神像，其功能类似于家庭守护神小雕像。这尊雕像置于一个平坦表面之上（可能是祭坛），它的前方摆放了一枝桃金娘。画面的前景展示了其他贡品：一盏盛有残酒的银杯、一只山羊头和一把青铜酒壶。贡品后方有一巨大岩石，上置一个带有铰链式把手的青铜托盘，其中盛满了各种水果，有松果、石榴、无花果和椰枣。

53

有马头像的酒壶
Wine Jug with Protome of a Horse

青铜
高 25 厘米，宽 13 厘米
公元 1 世纪
维苏威火山遗址
那不勒斯国家考古博物馆藏，编号 69083

Bronze
h 25 cm, w 13 cm
1st century CE
Vesuvian area
National Archaeological Museum of Naples,
inv. 69083

狮子和酒神游行场景马赛克
Mosaic with Lion and Dionysian Procession

马赛克
高 265 厘米，宽 265 厘米，厚 10 厘米
公元前 1 世纪
庞贝
那不勒斯国家考古博物馆藏，编号 10019

Mosaic
h 265 cm, w 265 cm, d 10 cm
1ˢᵗ century BCE
Pompeii
National Archaeological Museum of Naples, *inv. 10019*

这幅华丽的马赛克发掘于1829年，它位于一个宽敞餐厅的地面中央。这个奢华餐厅的四周墙面皆有壁画点缀，这些壁画属于庞贝第三风格，可追溯至奥古斯都时期。

马赛克由精巧多彩的叠褶纹样镶边，中间生动描绘了狄俄尼索斯祭坛的内部场景。画面中央是一头长着浓密鬃毛的雄狮，身上缠绕着花环，两只前爪戴着金镯。酒神狄俄尼索斯、他的女祭司们（Maenads）以及长着小翅膀的小爱神丘比特环绕在它的身边。这头神圣的野兽体型比周遭人物大了数倍，却温顺伏于院中，似是已被周遭狂欢的音乐和酒神的幻影所降服。

这件艺术品采用了"蠕虫状工艺"（opus vermiculatum），即使用仅3毫米大小的微型镶嵌砖紧密排列，铺成蜿蜒曲纹，精准勾勒出主体轮廓。马赛克上画面的原型可追溯至公元前1世纪，它直接参考了阿尔克西拉乌斯的雕塑作品《与丘比特嬉戏的雌狮》，该雕塑创造于公元前1世纪，曾被置于恺撒广场内。

55

酒神女祭司
Fresco with Maenad

彩绘壁画
高 75 厘米，宽 55.5 厘米，厚 8 厘米
公元 1 世纪
赫库兰尼姆
那不勒斯国家考古博物馆藏，编号 8835

Painted fresco
h 75 cm, w 55.5 cm, d 8 cm
1st century CE
Herculaneum
National Archaeological Museum of Naples, *inv. 8835*

绘有众神像的项链垂饰

Medallions with Portraits of the Gods

彩绘壁画
高 33 厘米，宽 91.5 厘米，厚 6 厘米
公元 1 世纪
赫库兰尼姆
那不勒斯国家考古博物馆藏，·编号 9129

Painted fresco
h 33 cm, w 91.5 cm, d 6 cm
1ˢᵗ century CE
Herculaneum
National Archaeological Museum of Naples, *inv. 9129*

戏剧面具
Marble mask

大理石
高 40 厘米，宽 34 厘米，厚 19 厘米
公元 1 世纪
庞贝
那不勒斯国家考古博物馆藏，编号 6613

Marble
h 40 cm, w 34 cm, d 19 cm
1st century CE
Pompeii
National Archaeological Museum of Naples, *inv. 6613*

古罗马人认为，追求物欲享乐是必要的，但人需要通过物质迈向更深刻的快乐，即精神层面的愉悦。戏剧的繁荣反映了这种需求。随着戏剧的流行，戏剧审美影响了包括雕塑在内的诸多艺术形式，其中尤为突出的就是悲剧中强烈冲突的塑造。对戏剧，尤其是悲剧的向往和追求极大程度上影响了古罗马人的人神观念与美学理念。

58

悲剧面具
Fresco with Tragic Mask

彩绘壁画
高 44.5 厘米，宽 80.5 厘米，厚 6 厘米
公元 1 世纪
庞贝
那不勒斯国家考古博物馆藏，编号 9792

Painted fresco
h 44.5 cm, w 80.5 cm, d 6 cm
1ˢᵗ century CE
Pompeii
National Archaeological Museum of Naples,
inv. 9792

59

面具壁画
Fresco with Mask

彩绘壁画
高 50 厘米，宽 74 厘米，厚 10 厘米
公元 1 世纪
赫库兰尼姆
那不勒斯国家考古博物馆藏，编号 9804

Painted fresco
h 50 cm, w 74 cm, d 10 cm
1ˢᵗ century CE
Herculaneum
National Archaeological Museum of Naples,
inv. 9804

III

美 的 演 绎

THE INTERPRETATION OF BEAUTY

《会饮篇》中，柏拉图借苏格拉底之口，将人们对美的追求进行了不同层次的剖析：从对形体之美的痴迷出发，进而追求灵魂之美中高尚品格的体现，最终升华至对美之本质的思索，爱则是这一切的驱动力。

古罗马艺术家们受希腊艺术与哲学启迪，通过雕塑、壁画深入探讨美的本质，对美进行了丰富的演绎。他们勾勒人体优美的曲线，展示和谐之美，描绘庄重的面容，传递至善的品格。他们打造出的艺术品承载了无数神话中浪漫的爱情故事，为后世留下了一份永恒之美的珍贵遗产。

In *Symposium*, Plato, through the mouth of Socrates, analyzed humanity's pursuit of beauty at different levels: beginning with the obsession with physical beauty, moving towards the pursuit of the noble character of the soul, and finally sublimating to the contemplation of the essence of beauty, with love as the driving force behind it all.

Inspired by Greek art and philosophy, artists in the Roman Empire sought to explore the essence of beauty through their works, including sculpture and frescoes, interpreting it in various ways. They captured the graceful curves of the human body, displaying the beauty of harmony, portrayed solemn faces, that reflected human virtues. Their art pieces carried numerous romantic love stories from myths, leaving a precious legacy of eternal beauty for future generations.

Going from one to two and from two to all beautiful bodies, and from
beautiful bodies to beautiful practices, and from beautiful practices to
beautiful kinds of knowledge, and from beautiful kinds of knowledge finally
to that particular knowledge which is knowledge solely of the beautiful itself,
so that at last, he may know what the beautiful itself really is.

— Plato, The Symposium

"从一个美的形体到两个美的形体，从两个美的形体到所有美的形体，从形体之美到体制之美，从体制之美到知识之美，最后再从知识之美进到仅以美本身为对象的那种学问，最终明白什么是美。"

——［古希腊］柏拉图《会饮篇》

维纳斯的背影
Statue of Venus Callipige

大理石
高 170 厘米，宽 48 厘米，厚 48 厘米
公元 2 世纪
罗马
那不勒斯国家考古博物馆藏，编号 6020

Marble
h 170 cm, w 48 cm, d 48 cm
2nd century CE
Rome
National Archaeological Museum of Naples, *inv. 6020*

　　这尊优雅的立柱维纳斯雕像展示了女神在沐浴前抬起长袍的姿态，表达了两种截然不同的美学观念：其一是女神体态的自然之美，其二是她在欣赏自己水中倒影时的满足。这件雕塑深受古希腊雕塑家普拉克西特列斯的影响，从全新的角度探讨了人与自然之间的关系。

61

手持七弦琴的阿波罗
Apollo Citharoedus

瓦迪哈马马特杂砂岩
高 244 厘米，宽 100 厘米，厚 76 厘米
公元 2 世纪
罗马
那不勒斯国家考古博物馆藏，编号 6262

Wadi Hammamat greywacke
h 244 cm, w 100 cm, d 76 cm
2nd century CE
Rome
National Archaeological Museum of Naples, *inv. 6262*

公爵奥多阿尔多·法尔内塞于1546年购得此雕像，并将其安置于罗马的法尔内塞宫。后来，它被带到那不勒斯的卡波迪蒙特宫展出，最终抵达那不勒斯国家考古博物馆展厅。太阳神兼艺术之神的阿波罗雕塑半裸，长袍从他身旁两侧垂落至华丽的凉鞋。他的目光望向左侧，七弦琴由左手托起并立于柱上，右臂高举于头顶，体现了古希腊雕塑家普拉克西特列斯对休憩时刻的人体的关注。

老普林尼在《自然史》中提到，本雕塑的原型是提马尔基得斯于公元前179年左右为阿波罗索西乌斯神庙创作的雕塑。本件则是公元2世纪制作的复制品。这一安敦尼时期的版本使用的材料再现了青铜的特质。

62

小屋大维娅
Female Statue with Portrait of Octavia Minor

大理石
高 203 厘米，宽 86 厘米，厚 70 厘米
公元 1 世纪
罗马
那不勒斯国家考古博物馆藏，编号 6125

Marble
h 203 cm, w 86 cm, d 70 cm,
1st century CE
Rome
National Archaeological Museum of Naples, *inv. 6125*

这位披着褶皱长袍的女性形象是朱里亚·克劳狄时女性朴素之美的理想典范。奥古斯都统治下的女性时尚反映出一种朴素化的审美回归，但这并未削弱女性形象的魅力与美感，尤其是体现在多种多样的发型上。

小屋大维娅是奥古斯都的姐姐。这尊以她为原型的雕像向我们展示了帝国早期的纪念性肖像特征，它也成为罗马公共建筑中最宏伟和最令人震撼的雕塑之一。

雅典娜

Statue of Athena-Minerva

帕罗斯大理石
高 197 厘米，宽 92 厘米，厚 52 厘米
公元 2 世纪
罗马
那不勒斯国家考古博物馆藏，编号 6321

Parian marble
h 197 cm, w 92 cm, d 52 cm
2nd century CE
Rome
National Archaeological Museum of Naples, *inv. 6321*

这尊雕像中的智慧女神雅典娜呈站立姿态。她以左腿为支撑，右腿向右伸展，右臂高举并握有长矛，这彰显了其战争之神的身份。这位诞生于宙斯头颅中的女神具有专属的典型特征，例如保护她左臂的盾牌和饰有美杜莎头像的盔甲。

光明女神黛安娜
Statue of Diana Lucifera

帕罗斯大理石
高 170 厘米，宽 77 厘米，厚 56 厘米
公元 2 世纪
来源未知
那不勒斯国家考古博物馆藏，编号 6280

Parian marble
h 170 cm, w 77 cm, d 56 cm
2nd century CE
Unknown
National Archaeological Museum of Naples, *inv. 6280*

尽管这座雕塑通常被认为是光明女神黛安娜，但实际上它也可以被视为月亮女神塞勒涅。依照传统形象，女神被描绘为降落到地面的姿态，她的披风在头顶扬起。在庞贝壁画中，女神出现在她钟爱的恩底弥翁面前似乎是众所周知的经典场景。雕像右手中的火炬是在近代修复过程中被人们添加上去的。

65

勒达与天鹅
Leda and the Swan

彩绘壁画
高 79 厘米，宽 84 厘米，厚 8 厘米
公元 1 世纪
庞贝
那不勒斯国家考古博物馆藏，编号 9550

Painted fresco
h 79 cm, w 84 cm, d 8 cm
1st century CE
Pompeii
National Archaeological Museum of Naples,
inv. 9550

66

纳西索斯
Narcissus

彩绘壁画
高 88 厘米，宽 74 厘米，厚 6 厘米
公元 1 世纪
庞贝
那不勒斯国家考古博物馆藏，编号 9388

Painted fresco
h 88cm, w 74 cm, d 6 cm
1ˢᵗ century CE
Pompeii
National Archaeological Museum of Naples, *inv. 9388*

英文中的"水仙"（Narcissus）和"自恋"（Narcissism）均由纳西索斯的名字而来。

在希腊神话中，纳西索斯是河神刻菲索斯与水泽神女利里俄珀的儿子。他的母亲从著名的先知忒瑞西阿斯那里得知，纳西索斯只有在不看到自己面容的情况下，才会长寿。因此，纳西索斯长大后虽然成为全希腊最俊美的男子，但他却从未看到过自己的容貌。

纳西索斯的美貌使人都为之倾倒，但他对前来求爱的人都漠不关心。所以，被拒绝的求爱者请求复仇女神涅墨西斯惩罚纳西索斯。涅墨西斯在知晓故事后，同意了他们的请求。一次，纳西索斯狩猎后口渴难耐，复仇女神便将他引诱到池水旁，在水中他看到了自己青春洋溢的倒影。纳西索斯在没有意识到这是自己的倒影的情况下，深深地爱上了它，却最终痛苦地意识到自己的爱无法得到回应。内心炽烈的激情之火将他融化，最终化作了一株金白相间的水仙花。

67

俯身的阿佛洛狄忒与厄洛斯
Crouching Aphroditewith Eros

大理石
高 140 厘米，宽 90 厘米，厚 60 厘米
公元 2 世纪
罗马
那不勒斯国家考古博物馆藏，编号 6293

Marble
h 140 cm, w 90 cm, d 60 cm
2ndcentury CE
Rome
National Archaeological Museum of Naples, *inv. 6293*

这尊描绘女神蹲姿梳洗场景的雕塑，最初是由更具延展性的材料（青铜）制作而成，创作时期晚于另一雕塑作品《维纳斯的背影》。其呈现出的女神向下蜷曲的身姿，展现了古希腊雕塑家普拉克西特列斯对神圣之美思索的演变。这一形象的原型由比提尼亚（今土耳其）的雕塑家代达沙斯所创作，是为其国王尼科美德一世所作的皇室委托艺术品。在罗马时期，这一形象广泛流行，无数复制品被用于装饰别墅和宫殿花园。

结　语

"形色，天性也；惟圣人，然后可以践形。"

——《孟子·尽心上》

　　与苏格拉底的《大希庇阿斯篇》大抵同时，中国的儒家贤者孟子也曾对"美"进行论述。他认为，外在的美需要圣人般的德行来支撑。一东一西，两位先贤对"美"本质的结论或许有所差异，但都将其归因于人类共通的、跨越物质表象的精神世界。

　　展览中的古罗马文物是西方美学之至宝，鲜明地呈现了这个伟大文明的审美追求与标准。这些文物在时空上与此地今时遥不可及，却能让我们在观赏时，无碍地欣赏、理解、认同古罗马人对"美"的表现与追求，并启发我们对自身文化、历史的思考与珍视。这种思考与珍视是人类不同文明之间的惺惺相惜，也是文化交流能够带给观众最重要的意义。

Conclusion

The bodily organs with their functions belong to our Heaven-conferred nature. But a man must be a sage before he can satisfy the design of his bodily organization.

—— *Menius, Jin Xin I*

Around the same time as Plato's *Hippias Major*, Chinese Confucian scholar Mencius also discussed "beauty" in his work. He believed that external beauty requires the moral character of a sage to support it. From East to West, the conclusions of these two sages on the essence of "beauty" may differ, but both attribute it to a common, transcendent spiritual world of humanity that goes beyond material appearances.

The ancient Roman artifacts in the exhibition are the treasures of Western aesthetics, vividly presenting the aesthetic pursuits and standards of this great civilization. Although these artifacts are far from us in both time and space, they allow us to unobstructedly appreciate, understand, and identify with the ancient Romans' expression and pursuit of "beauty", and inspire us to think about and cherish our own culture and history. This reflection and cherishing is a mutual understanding between different civilizations and represents the most important meaning that cultural exchange can bring to the audience.

指导单位

中国文物交流中心

北京歌华传媒集团有限责任公司

主办单位

北京歌华文化发展集团有限公司

中华世纪坛艺术馆

意大利那不勒斯国家考古博物馆

联合主办单位

意大利驻华大使馆

意大利驻华使馆文化处

意大利 MONDO MOSTRE 公司

承办单位

北京歌华文化中心有限公司

北京坤远文博展览有限公司

展览中方组织委员会

中方学术顾问　丁宁（北京大学教授）

总制作　肖红　黄春雷

总策划　马龙　冀鹏程

总统筹　刘冰　许波

中方策展人　王昭祎　戴鹏伦

展览统筹　王猛　洪夏

展览策划　蒋海梅　刘妍言

展陈设计　梁潇

平面设计　冯帆　魏琦

内容文案　刘家朋　林筱音　顾赫然

国际联络　刘妍言　孙思萌

宣传推广　庄园　王清　毕敬颖　马晓旭　马天怡
　　　　　李凯　岳聪　孙婷

公共教育　季楠　吕康　秦丽杰　郑朝阳　康可儿

展览运营　梁辰　薛智中　宋九一　唐英哲　梦洋

CURATOR OF THE EXHIBITION Mario Grimaldi

Colophon MANN
Museo Archeologico Nazionale Di Napoli

MUSEUM DIRECTOR Paolo Giulierini
DIRECTOR'S OFFICE Patrizia Cilenti
ADMINISTRATIVE DEPARTMENT Stefania Saviano
SCIENTIFIC DIRECTION – ARTWORK CONSERVATION
Laura Forte, Marialucia Giacco, Floriana Miele
Emanuela Santaniello, Giovanni Vastano
EXHIBITIONS DEPARTMENT
Laura Forte, Marialucia Giacco
ARCHIVAL AND PHOTOGRAPHIC DEPARTMENT
Laura Forte
CATALOGUING DEPARTMENT Floriana Miele
COMMUNICATION, MEDIA RELATIONS, MARKETING
AND FUNDRAISING DEPARTMENT Antonella Carlo
LEGAL DEPARTMENT Luigi Di Caprio
MUSEOLOGY AND HISTORICAL DOCUMENTATION
DEPARTMENT Andrea Milanese
RESTORATION DEPARTMENT Mariateresa Operetto
EDUCATIONAL SERVICES, RESEARCH, PROMOTION
AND VALORISATION DEPARTMENT Giovanni Vastano
TECHNICAL DEPARTMENT Amanda Piezzo

THANKS TO
Elena Camerlingo, Ruggiero Ferrajoli, Alessandro Gioia, Angela
Luppino, Caterina Serena Martucci, Amelia Menna, Vittoria Minniti,
Maria Morisco, Quintina Napolano, Ciro Palladino, Luciano and
Marco Pedicini, Anna Pizza, Giovanna Scarpati, Ciro Spina, Giovanna
Stingone, Manuela Valentini, Serena Venditto, the Protocol Bureau,
the Surveillance Coordinators, and all MANN staff.

Italian Side participated by
MONDO MOSTRE

PRESIDENT Tomaso Radaelli
CEO Simone Todorow di San Giorgio
HEAD OF INTERNATIONAL BUSINESS Maria Azzurra La Rosa
HEAD OF LEGAL & COMPANY AFFAIRS Chiara Ferraro
HEAD OF EXHIBITIONS-ASIA Stefano Silvani
EXHIBITION MANAGER Elisa Faggio
ADMINISTRATION AND GENERAL AFFAIRS Stefano Martino

图书在版编目(CIP)数据

古罗马文明之光：意大利那不勒斯国家考古博物馆珍藏/中华世纪坛艺术馆，北京坤远文博展览有限公司编.—上海：上海书画出版社，2023.6
ISBN 978-7-5479-3115-8

Ⅰ.①古… Ⅱ.①中… ②北… Ⅲ.①文物-古罗马-图录 Ⅳ.①K885.46

中国国家版本馆CIP数据核字（2023）第084861号

古罗马文明之光：
意大利那不勒斯国家考古博物馆珍藏

The Light of Ancient Roman Civilization:
Masterpieces From the National Archaeological Museum of Naples

中华世纪坛艺术馆　北京坤远文博展览有限公司 编

责任编辑	王聪荟
审　读	王　剑
装帧设计	陈绿竞
技术编辑	包赛明

出版发行	上 海 世 纪 出 版 集 团
	上海书画出版社
地址	上海市闵行区号景路159弄A座4楼
邮政编码	201101
网址	www.shshuhua.com
E-mail	shcpph@163.com
制版	上海久段文化发展有限公司
印刷	浙江新华印刷技术有限公司
经销	各地新华书店
开本	889×1194　1/16
印张	7.5
版次	2023年6月第1版　2023年6月第1次印刷
书号	**ISBN 978-7-5479-3115-8**
定价	**198.00元**

若有印刷、装订质量问题，请与承印厂联系